About the author

Pat Williams was director of the London College of Storytellers and works as a writer, lecturer and human givens therapist. She co-authored a best-selling encyclopaedia of human beliefs and more recently wrote *King Kong – Our Knot of Time and Music: A personal memoir of South Africa's legendary musical,* published in 2017 by Granta Books.

In her regular column for *Human Givens,* the journal of the Human Givens Institute, she explores a wide range of new ideas and information relating to human behaviour and experience. Her popular workshop *How to tell Stories that Heal,* designed for the Human Givens College, aims at the psychotherapeutic, caring and educational professions.

She has also produced two informative MP3s; *How Stories Heal: the effect of stories on mental health and human development,* and *Which You are You…? Our many minds and how to manage them,* both of which are available for download from Human Givens Publishing's website.

Just Looking

Also by the author

King Kong – Our Knot of Time and Music: A personal
memoir of South Africa's legendary musical

Which you are you...? Our many minds
and how to manage them (MP3)

How Stories Heal – the effects of stories on mental
health and human development (MP3)

Co-authored with Douglas Hill

The Supernatural: An encylopaedia of human belief

Just Looking

upstream and
downstream

by Pat Williams

Human Givens
Publishing

Human Givens
Publishing

For
Daud jān
with gratitude,
always

and for
Gill Whitworth
with boundless gratitude

CONTENTS

Introduction

THE ESSAYS in this book are a selection from the 'Pat Williams Pages' published either in *The Therapist*, *The New Therapist*, or the *Human Givens* Journal between 1996 and 2018. My brief to myself was simply to find an idea that interested me and then explore it, keeping the writing entertaining and anecdotal, and remaining mindful of the fact that the majority of readers would be working in either psychotherapy (as I do) or education. Though what I wrote reads, I hope, as a light glide across the surfaces, I also tried to build further thoughts into the text, should a reader choose to unpack them.

Writing to a fixed length is an absurd task. My first drafts were sometimes nearly twice as long as the finished product, and then painstakingly cut and condensed to fit the available space. It was a frustrating process, though satisfying in its way, because although so many words had to be jettisoned, the thoughts they carried somehow held on, stuck there in spite of the intense compression. My husband David, who from time to time crops up in these pages, characterises this intensive process of winnowing words without losing the meaning as 'homeopathic writing'.

Now that these pieces are collected in one place, I can see how strong my early South African background and experiences have been in forming my attitudes and perceptions and understandings. They frequently provided, in Goethe's memorable phrase, 'an instance worth a thousand, bearing all within itself'. I see, too, that I seem to have been writing the same piece over and over again, in different guises. This has been partly because, as in any series of conversations extending over years, willy-nilly we repeat ourselves, revealing our preoccupations even to ourselves. And what clearly shows itself in these collected pieces are the questions that I, like many others, have been asking most of my life: "What's really going on in this baffling world in which we find ourselves? What can therapists and educators and others learn from simply looking underneath the appearance of, or our current explanations for, this or that?"(One of the many formative things I learned from my early life living in the apartheid era was that by looking underneath and around the appearances rather than from above, we can see more – just as our disenfranchised servants observed and understood more about their masters than we, the masters, knew about ourselves or them.)

Over the years I have learned that light is best shed on the questions we contemplate by means of metaphor, analogy, stories or jokes. I hope you will enjoy the ones you find in these collected 'Pages'.

I

The shifting sands
of the Dialogue

MANY YEARS AGO I showed a friend's paintings to the owner of a fashionable and successful art gallery. Each picture, it seemed to me, while conventionally 'representational', sang with a truth and inevitability that hinted at 'something more'.

The gallery owner agreed the painter was very good, exceptionally good, even. "But I can't show this work", she told me. "Why not?" "Because," said this woman, encapsulating hours of art talk in a sentence, "it's outside the Dialogue".

I didn't understand then. But as time went on, her words explained many puzzles, and not only about the art world. From trivial fashions to publishing, from politics and education to scientific theory, from religious beliefs to transcendent speculations, very little, I came to realise, is free of the Dialogue's constraints.

For a period of time, any particular Dialogue is 'where it's at': the dominant universe of discourse. It determines what's acceptable and what excluded; what's visible and what we are blind to. Try to offer something else, as I did with my friend's paintings, and you can seem hopelessly out-of-touch or perhaps even a little mad. Indeed, when professions share intentions, but have divergent Dialogues (as is the case, say, with orthodox medicine and homeopathy) in most respects they will reject each other.

About 60 years ago the entrenched idea that people did monstrous things because of inherent wickedness began to be challenged. Arendt introduced the fundamental yet instantly plausible idea of 'the banality of evil'. Asch, Milgram and Zimbardo designed ground-breaking studies demonstrating something most of us really weren't aware of at the time – just how easily the human mind was manipulated, and how 'decent' individuals could in certain circumstances be induced to do 'evil' things. Their work introduced a new Dialogue, which informed and broadened our perspective.

ıable ideas and findings of these former young Turks
ıg challenged by a new generation of contenders, all
ay at the idea that "tyranny triumphs because people
blı͜ ͜ ıow orders". One such group, for example, says that
recent studies, in particular studies of the Nazi regime, reveal that
its functionaries engaged "actively and creatively" with their tasks,
and that such behaviour can hardly then be called "mindless".

Setting aside the question of whether this fundamentally contradicts
current understanding (after all, 'creativity' is often harnessed to
objectives which themselves could be called 'blind' and 'mindless',
such as keeping your job or staying alive) I can detect here at least
as much power-seeking as truth-seeking. This is predictable. A new
Dialogue is waiting in the wings – increasingly impatiently.

Vaclav Havel's brilliant play, *The Memorandum*, satirises this
process. An organization deliberately introduces an artificial
language, called *Ptydepe*, in order "to streamline communication".
Ptydepe is awful – complex, arbitrary, bristling with rules, ruthlessly
logical but actually insane, and far from streamlining communication,
ultimately causes its complete breakdown. The play traces *Ptydepe's*
effect on the individuals in the office, and the power games its
introduction sets in play. Then as abruptly as it arrived, *Ptydepe* is
withdrawn, replaced by an equally crazy new language in which the
rules are reversed.

Although Havel's subtle and funny play is about communist
Czechoslovakia 60 years ago, it also illuminates something universal
– the fact that Dialogues are built on shifting sands. But while
they are in place, seemingly fixed and stable, those who control
them have power over everything from status to survival. Indeed
the function of brainwashing, whether formal or informal, is to
lock its victims into their masters' Dialogue. That, I think, is why
the tabloid British press is so callous: it has the power to be so,
having commandeered a Dialogue and rewritten the rules. In the
name of "our duty to our readers" and an ersatz moralism – "Love-
rat!" "Whore!", "Disgrace!" – gossip often masquerades as news,
reputations are destroyed, facts twisted, and innocent people hurt.
"But that's what we do!' said a tabloid editor in surprise, when it
was put to her that vulnerable people could be damaged by her

newspaper's treatment of them. No arguing with their Dialogue.

However in spite of such distortions, many new Dialogues can be useful. They can prod us out of old habits, reorganise our perceptions, help us examine assumptions, move us forward. But we do need the agility to slip under their fences when we choose.

Perhaps the best way to escape is simply to refuse to play, I remember a delightful moment on radio during the BBC's *Today* programme, on the first morning of a round of peace talks between Palestinians and Israelis, when a French diplomat declined to be drawn into discussing Iran. "I'm not going to comment on that." he said, "I'm enjoying myself this morning. This is a day for optimism". The journalist pushed and needled him, but the diplomat was unbudgeable: "Go and find someone else to talk about those things."

Dialogue, according to my dictionary, is a conversation most often between two people – and perhaps, by extension, between two opposing views. So a sub-category of Dialogue is, of course, Debate. These days we are constantly urged to it. "Join the debate, folks!" we hear on all sides. "Tell us what you think!" "Have your say!"

But debate is simply a way of seeing which 'side' has the bigger numbers, which point of view will prevail, who can make the cleverest case. It is also a cheap way of filling airtime and newsprint, in the cynical knowledge that our 'say', once said, will not be taken seriously and will never be heard again.

For debate takes you nowhere. You can't nose your way into ambiguities and uncertainties with debate. You can't even pretend you are looking for understanding. Where can truth be found in debate between just two opposing 'sides'? Collapsed on the floor somewhere, I think, weak and gagging. And at the same time serenely shining, remote from the reductionism of the debate, yet as near as our very breath. Debate is a mere swinging pendulum. Truth holds the pattern.

In spite of the Dialogue's noise, however, from time to time we fall into a truer, subtler, more natural, and richer world; a world which is also, in the best sense, more ordinary. And then suddenly the daily Dialogues of our paper-thin culture disappear. It can happen, perhaps, when we are on the road, our mind idling, or so busy that we have no time to 'think', or when we are drenched in the beauty of a place, or listening to a story, or experiencing something for the first time. Such simple, personal experiences, and the sense of connectedness (and relief!) which accompanies them, are beyond any Dialogue and certainly not debatable.

Indeed, when art is required to fit the Dialogue (as with the paintings of my friend) the artist is effectively caged. And whenever that happens, whether to art or to anything else, then black or white, win or lose, 'on message' or out in the wilderness, the binary system has created us in its own image.

2

Good manners are
our best guide

GHANDI once said, when asked about Western Civilisation, that yes it would be a good idea. So too, I think, would cultural literacy.

Norwegian journalist Asne Seierstad's bestselling *The Bookseller of Kabul* provides a case in point. After covering the war in northern Afghanistan, Seierstad travelled to Kabul and spent hours in the bookseller's shop, hearing his stories about how he battled to survive the successive regimes, Soviet, mujaheddin and Taliban, and realising "he was a living piece of Afghan cultural history". Then she was invited for a meal with the family, and thought: "How interesting it would be to write a book about this family". Next day she told the bookseller her wish and here, from her preface to that book, is their total exchange:

"'Thank you' was all he said.

'But this means I would have to come and live with you'.

'You are welcome'.

'I would have to go around with you, live the way you live. With you, your wives, sisters, sons.'

'You are welcome', he repeated."

And so she came, long enough to research her book, privy to everything that went on in the family. She says she shared many good times. But hardly pausing to give that idea weight, she continues in the very same sentence: "but I have rarely been as angry as I was with the Khan family, and I have rarely quarrelled as much as I did there. Nor have I had the urge to hit anyone as much as I did there. The same thing was continually provoking me, the manner in which men treated women."

The bookseller is now suing Seierstad and her publisher for what he says were lies, distortions and dangerous indiscretions. There were "lots of misrepresentations of me, my family and my country", he says, adding that she did not understand that he was her host, and what that implied. He was "terribly terribly shocked... I very kindly accepted her, I gave my hospitality to her.... She doesn't understand how shameful it is to write such things on paper."

When we travel we tend to leave the baggage of our own problems behind, but very often, through lack of experience or imagination, we lug our cultural assumptions with us – and also underestimate the difficulties of the people we meet. The bookseller, trying to cope in an uncertain, explosive society and carrying the burden of responsibility for the safety of his family, found his guest's indiscretions 'dangerous'. For her part, Ms Seierstad was probably unaware of the effect she was having, and reacted much as she would have done in the West, against circumstances in which she had nothing to lose, much to gain, and in any case would soon leave behind.

I'm sure she felt herself to be well-intentioned, and that the bookseller was probably in some ways no better than he should have been. But her book is a seemingly impersonal, third-person story of a family, told as if she had not even been there. It has the aura of absolute truth that authorial omnipotence bestows, without a trace of the warmth or humour she must have experienced while being among her host's family. It is only from that single passage in her preface that we even know how turbulent her own emotions were – and as most readers will be aware, emotional arousal makes for very crude and stupid thinking,

Driven, then, by emotion, an unquestioningly 'western' agenda and the irresistible (to a journalist) momentum of 'a good story', the author crashed against all Afghan customs concerning the responsibilities laid on hosts and guests. It would have been dishonourable, indeed impossible, once she had asked for hospitality, that she should be refused ('thank you' and 'you are welcome' are repeated here, impassively, like the cultural mantras they are) and impossible too that the terms of her stay should be a matter for bargaining. Hospitality, when requested, is mandatory, no matter how poor or disadvantaged the host.

But the cultural expectation that goes with the requirements of such open-handedness is that it will not be abused. It is taken for granted that the guest will not stay too long (at the most three days), will respect the host, and will not violate the family's privacy. And though most of us would agree that the women in the family had (in our terms) few rights and faced severe limitations, they had also been kept safe through the atrocities of many turbulent years, and I doubt whether advertising their dilemmas has helped them now.

We have all heard stories of cultural misunderstanding. Hippy children of rich consumer societies abused Afghan hospitality terribly in the 1970s, taking advantage of those who had so much less than they, moving in and staying on and on. And we see on TV soldiers manhandling women as they search houses in Iraq, not realising the taboos they are shattering, and the deep shock and violation the women feel.

Cultural literacy in today's world has become an elementary necessity. But it takes time, information and experience to acquire, and if we lack these elements, then how can we proceed with sensitivity?

Well, the human race long ago developed a wonderfully effective way, so gentle and subtle that it is often heedlessly brushed aside as inconsequential. It is, simply, good manners. Scoffed at, derided by sophisticates and yobs alike – and yet pure gold.

Game theory, I'm told, demonstrates that the most successful winning strategy is to give the other person the benefit of the doubt – unless or until you see that the doubt is justified. So you could almost call good manners the social application of game theory.

Or you could see good manners as diplomacy, that interface between nations, but at an individual level. Each of us is a separate culture – a sovereign country, so to speak. The integrity of our borders should be respected, and entry therein courteously and attentively negotiated.

Good manners help us to know how we should behave, and never more so than when unfamiliar customs or contexts bewilder or upset us. They hold a situation, keeping surfaces equable while we explore what is going on and what may be possible, rather than diving in with wrong assumptions. They give us time to learn step by step what another person or group is like – to find and share in the other's humanity, if possible, and then proceed from there. And they can continue to hold us, the more we learn and the deeper we go into any situation or relationship. They keep resentment, negativity and greed in check. They regard the powerful and the vulnerable as equally deserving of consideration.

And at their most profound, they shade into chivalry, generosity – and wisdom.

3

Thoughts from
the cliff-edge

LEMMING JOKES seem to be everywhere right now. You may have heard some, or seen the cartoons. *Private Eye* shows the lemmings tumbling down the cliff edge, one saying to another as they fall: "What do you mean, Plan B?" A *New Yorker* cartoon has two scientists watching a scramble of lemmings flying *up* the cliff edge. The one scientist explains to his colleague: "We crossed them with salmon". And another journal shows a lemming in free fall wearing a neat little parachute and a blissful smile.

We've probably all seen film of these charming cousins of hamsters, voles and rats hurtling over the edge of cliffs into the sea in an apparently meaningless rush to suicide. Indeed this image has become a metaphor for what happens when we, too, all rush down a disastrous path just because everybody else is.

The truth about the lemmings, however, is *not* as we believe it to be. Their headlong leap into sea or river is now understood to be a biological compulsion towards mass migration. Instead of obeying an irresistible urge to destroy themselves, they are actually making a frantic bid for survival. When their environment becomes unsustainable, they race to get the hell out. Do they realise, do they even care, how far the drop down the cliff might be, how sharp the rocks they could get splattered on? Lemmings can swim, and those lucky enough to find dry land before they drown from exhaustion can start a new colony and carry right on.

Misconceptions about lemmings go back many centuries. In the 1530s, the geographer known as Zeigler of Strasbourg proposed the theory that the creatures fell out of the sky during stormy weather and then died suddenly when the grass grew in spring. This was challenged by the Danish natural historian Ole Worm, who acknowledged that though lemmings *could* possibly fall out of the sky it was more likely they were brought over by the wind.

The idea of mass suicide, however, arose in our own times. It seems to have taken hold through a 1958 Walt Disney film, *White Wilderness*, which won a 'best documentary feature' Academy Award. I remember seeing it, and the massed migrating throng, and their jump to certain death, remain vivid in my mind. But it turns out those scenes were callously and ingeniously faked. The lemmings in the film were flown 2,000 miles across Canada, from Hudson Bay to Calgary, where far from willingly jumping off a cliff, they were launched off it by means of a turntable.

This cruel and bogus footage, combined with quite usual but very abrupt fluctuations in the population of Norwegian lemmings, seems to be the source of the perception which has so gripped our minds that it has now become folklore. We have, in fact, created the metaphor we need. For even though untrue, we know, deeply know, that in the really real world, that is to say the metaphorical world, these lovable little creatures *must* destroy themselves. Their seemingly meaningless rush to doom resonates very deeply with the intense and familiar human fear of being caught up and swept along by forces, and in directions, completely beyond our control. We can easily imagine that we too may be tipped over the edge into the murky seas of our species' Lowest Common Denominator.

But this is what is happening to us in any case! From cradle to grave we are swept along, swept along – subject to the winds that blow. Born into and moulded by family and society, we are in the hands of others from the start, enclosed in predetermined ways of seeing, and being in, the world. We are obliged to live with the consequences of often insane decisions taken by those who prefer status and power over sense or knowledge. We are taken into wars even when we are among millions protesting against them. We may vote for representatives who, right through our lifetimes, are never chosen. And in our final years we may find ourselves tidied away, if we are unlucky, into some cruel indifference currently called 'Care'. Such is life within our benign democracy. Under dictatorships it is inconceivably worse.

In bleaker moments it often seems to me as if we are at a point where almost anything could precipitate destruction's tipping point. A domino effect could be caused by lack of petrol, shortage of food, more millions unemployed, or the collapse of our increasingly pervasive, increasingly precarious, information systems. Maybe we will reap the whirlwind of too many of our leaders' mistakes over too many years. Maybe we'll be destroyed by that damn butterfly flapping its wings on the other side of the planet.

We fear all of the above, because we do not see how any of it might be stopped. And fear turns most of us into animals. Indeed, contemplating all the forces outside us over which we have no control, as well as the large animal component within us, I wonder how on earth the human race has managed to survive thus far, and can only conclude that a sufficient amount of 'something else' must be at work. Indeed, it seems to me that some of the signposts to that 'something else' are very close to us indeed, sitting there – within humanity's stories, for instance – waiting for the penny to drop.

Indeed, many traditional tales illustrate our animal tendencies very precisely. And they show us, too, that these can be withstood, that we can choose to connect with that part of ourselves which is subtler than either the world outside or the animal within. Without much fuss, at certain moments, we find we can stand our ground, walk away, say "no, not today". The trick is to pick our time. And when we do, we know a feeling of relaxation and quiet clarity utterly different from the strain of dancing to someone else's tune.

I think about the mass exodus of the lemmings and wonder if they too, as we, are led over the cliff by the foolhardy, the ambitious, the thrill-seekers and the mad, all just hoping that their impulse to head for the edge and brave the long drop into unknown waters will turn out OK, in the short term anyway. And sometimes it does.

But what interests me most of all is that even as they rush to the cliff edge, not all lemmings take the plunge. Whenever I've watched the film footage, I always notice a number of them peeling off at the edges of the pack and scurrying off in a different direction.

4

There's always something behind it

DID YOU KNOW – I have it on very dubious authority – that the late Princess Diana was part of the Diana cult which has existed since Roman times, and that William and Harry therefore have divine blood? Or that the Masters of the New World Order objected to Dodi Fayed because they had someone else in mind for Diana to marry, namely Bill Clinton? It would have been necessary for him to divorce or kill Hilary, of course. But this sacrifice was not called for, because Diana refused and therefore had to die. And her death, the same source assures me, was brought about by means of a satanic rite performed by the British royal family. And did all that grab your attention?

It grabbed mine when I found it, and I wonder if – apart from its obvious entertainment value – that was because human beings are so primed to ask questions and look beyond surfaces that even this kind of nonsense will momentarily pull us up short.

Trawl the Web and you will find that virtually every notable event in the past century has produced a conspiracy theory. World War I was a Jewish conspiracy. The events of 9/11 were perpetrated by President Bush. The collapse of Baring's Bank bears the secret hand of the Pope. Roosevelt and Hitler were in cahoots right through World War II. The U.S. deliberately caused the Asian tsunami by detonating an undersea bomb. The "Iraqi Republican Guard" intended to maroon then destroy the American Army inside Iraq. And you and me are unwitting victims of new media mind control technology, including a "colour-coded language" fired straight down our optic nerve.

What are we to make of all this? Well, on the principle that we can do nothing about the conspiracies but plenty about ourselves, I think the most useful thing is to see them as magnifying mirrors of the condition in which, willy-nilly, we find ourselves.

We humans hate being at the mercy of the unknown. Thrown here as we are, our primary instinct is to make coherent the chaos in which we've landed. We question everything that might affect us either intimately or from a distance – questions from "what the hell am I doing here anyway?" to "is he telling the truth?" to "is there a lion behind that bush?" One of the very few things we are sure of is that there's always something behind it, whatever "it" happens to be.

In humanity's early days we told stories to explain the unknown forces around us. Many superstitions, and some glorious metaphorical tales, were the result. The myths, characterised by their scope and grandeur, accounted for forces and events which could not be gainsaid, and allowed us to hold firm in the face of the unknown. The superstitions, which assigned meaning to unconnected events, joining up the dots with threads of ignorance, fear and desire, were perhaps our earliest conspiracy theories.

Remote from those days of innocence, the ignorance that unsettles us today is largely of our own making. We are playthings of our artefacts, lost in an accelerating confetti of systems and disjointed information. Apart from those stories we accept from science and religion, either because they suit us or else because we respect their 'authority', we still feel at the mercy of the unknown and still make up stories to give us a sense of control – because in the words of Bob Dylan: "… something's happening, and you don't know what it is, do you, Mr Jones?"

Just as Ulysses' wife Penelope, in the *Odyssey*, spun and unravelled tapestries to keep her suitors at bay, so too at every level of life, from the disasters within and between nations, to the highest human hopes and aspirations, the truth is similarly veiled, appearing and disappearing before our eyes.

Looking no further than our own society we find shameful realities – land and water secretly poisoned, child abuse covered up by "men of God", corporations hiding vast frauds, wars undertaken on a lie, deliberate distortion posing as public information, and a lack of honour so widespread that much of the time we'd be right to assume that everyone in a position of power is lying, manipulating for their own purposes both public opinion and public anxiety. Who can we trust? No wonder we suspect the existence of cover-ups. We think people do get "disposed of". And when we hint publicly at the possibility of dirty work, some smug bastard with too much power will say: "that's just a conspiracy theory. You're not one of *those* are you?"

Certainly the wacky ones give the others a bad name – and this could even be the point. Conspiracy theories may most of the time be the result of paranoia – but in other cases could actually be deliberate disinformation. The truth, buried within a tangle of lies, plausible invention and real facts, turns into a far-fetched joke.

The confusion – and I imagine we've all experienced it – is further compounded by the nature of our own minds. We are trapped by assumptions, expectations, fantasies, beliefs and desires, as well as the unreliability of our senses, just as much as we are by the skewed or deliberate misinformation we are fed. Conspiracy and cover-ups compound the illusion, but even without them we are like demented travellers in private trains, peering out of separate windows and locked into what we think we see. Even the simplest newspaper report never tallies with the experience of someone who was there.

No wonder so many of us feel that life as we generally know it is a pantomime; a charade; a dream. The categories, the realities, are not as described.

It seems to me that whatever appears on the screen of our consciousness is like a film of events, selectively shot and then cut and edited – a fiction which touches reality only at certain points. But reality itself includes what the "film version" misses – what ends up on the cutting room floor, and what happens behind the cameras.

Yet we are not helpless. The survival instinct planted so deeply within us to seek answers, find out, solve problems, will prompt the right questions. The trick is to try not to fool ourselves. Occasionally, we even manage it. Here detachment is paramount. The less attached we are to an idea or piece of information, the more we can switch focus and increase the potential for clarity.

We need to discriminate between knowledge, fact, contention, theory, and opinion, knowing each for what it is. We need to take care not to "get off" on knowing something that others don't. And we need to be patient as detectives, inspecting ourselves for paranoia or bias, until we become like clear-eyed outsiders – or even visitors from another planet. And there have always been plenty of conspiracy theories about *them*.

5

"Children guessed, but only a few and down they forgot as up they grew"

FROM E.E. CUMMINGS'
ANYONE LIVED IN A PRETTY HOW TOWN

"REALITY", said Einstein, "is an illusion, albeit a persistent one". We're all caught in it, but those least in its thrall are children. It takes time (and teaching) to train them into the illusion, but until then they seem effortlessly and joyfully in tune with truths mostly lost to us as adults. Indeed the delight of talking to children is not only the pleasure of connecting with their purity and directness, but also because they draw us back to that same state in ourselves. I've thought for years that along with pens, paper and glasses of water, a few babies should be placed in their carry-chairs on the tables at summit meetings, peace conferences – and, given recent events, at conclaves of bankers too.

Every culture's proverbs, I imagine, encapsulate the clear-sightedness of children. We quote the Bible: "out of the mouths of babes and sucklings..." Afghans, my husband David tells me, say: "If you want the truth, ask a child". If there's an elephant in the room, a child will see it. If the emperor suddenly has no clothes, a child will know it. Perhaps that is why Hans Anderson's story strikes such an immediate chord in us: we all have our own emperor, our own courtiers, our own illusory clothes – and our own child. And perhaps that is why, too, *The Reason I Jump*, the book by autistic author Naoki Higashida, is so valuable. Because he wrote it when still a child, he was still able to communicate the naked truths of his awareness. Twenty years later he may have become just another nerd, those intense inner experiences all but forgotten.

Yet certain fragments of a clarity generally lost to the adult world remain in us all I think, usually undisclosed but forever treasured. I wrote to various friends recently asking if this was as true of them as it is of me, and indeed each had one or two such memories they could recall. One of the most consistent was of the luminous vividness of colour as if, in the words of one of them, we had extra receptors in our eyes, seeing (in Wordsworth's words) "meadow, grove and stream ... apparelled in celestial light". Another was the immediacy of music. One friend recalled that listening to live music affected her so powerfully that she kept experiencing fleeting moments of unconsciousness, however hard she fought against them.

An interesting picture emerged. A therapist spoke of the insight, at about seven, when her mother was very angry with her: "that's not my mother speaking, it's just the anger talking". A poet knew, with complete certainty, when he was four, that adults were disproportionately upset about death and that there was absolutely no need to be. He felt duty bound to reassure them, but didn't quite know how to go about it. An artist said he had the ability to approach dangerous stray dogs, feral cats, and birds, "because I had a great love for them, and identified with them". He could also sense – as several others mentioned too – tensions and blocks in people's bodies. "When I was about five I knew instinctively how to massage my father by walking on his back", he said. Another spoke of "just seeing" where friends' tensions and pains were, and then 'rubbing' them away.

Energy fields were sometimes mentioned, electric feelings often in fingers and hands. "I even caused the TV to fuse when my mum interrupted something I was watching", said one. "And I did that kind of thing more than once". Another was scared when, aged seven, walking to school, she encountered an invisible but steady column of energy at a point on the pavement, which seemed to descend from above and plunge on down through the earth. She tried each day to avoid it, because when she accidentally stepped within it she was gripped and held by the zinging strength of the 'current'.

Above all, everyone remembered strong reactions against hypocrisy, particularly in religion. A software engineer said that at the age of about five he realised that the religious people he met were all lying, because if they were telling the truth they would be behaving quite differently. The artist said he had hysterics when his parents brought a priest to their house. "I just didn't want anything to do with that person". And a painter, growing up in Zambia, was told by a nun when she was eight that everyone, including her, would burn in hell unless they became Catholics. "When I said what about the remote people who might never see a missionary, the nun said everyone would get a chance sometime in their life. Which was so totally irrational that I realised it could only be her truth, not the real truth."

A designer remembered a couple coming to tea when he was nine, "very different from the people I was used to, who tended to be either extended family or in politics or the arts. "The man was a banker, and I vividly remember watching him being funny and entertaining, all animated and smiling. But I could see, really see, his hidden face underneath the smiles, which was distorted and ugly. I told my Mom I wouldn't come down from my room next time he visited, as I didn't like or trust him. A few years later he cheated the family out of a lot of money."

A man who grew up in Berlin told me: "None of the adults seemed to know what was happening to the Jews in Nazi Germany. In fact after the war they seemed genuinely surprised to hear about their fate. But we kids – we all knew." Another friend's memory, aged about four at the time, provides a gloss on this: "I saw adults ignoring all kinds of things which to me were quite obvious, and decided this must be some mysterious game everyone was playing, which I was supposed to learn. So I did – rather too well, I'm afraid".

Coincidentally, shortly after collecting these responses from my friends, research was published in the journal *Infancy*, demonstrating that infants detect hypocrisy even before they have language. "Adults often try to shield infants from distress by putting on a happy face following a negative experience. But babies know the truth: as early as 18 months, they can implicitly understand which emotions go with which events," says researcher Professor Diane Poulin-Dubois.

In fact I would surmise that some babies are aware of emotional inconsistencies even younger. One friend spoke of her puzzlement when, as a baby, she lay on the bed next to her sick mother, watching her aunt sympathising with her, and giving her a kiss. "I didn't understand why my mother couldn't see she was lying, and actually hated her."

It is a truism that our children are our future. But do we know how crucial they are to the present? It's as if, between them all, wherever they are, they hold, share and represent truths most adults have forgotten, thus acting as a battery, energising and brightening the planet. They are natural initiates into life's mysteries. In time they will inevitably be drawn into the "persistent illusion" Einstein speaks of, but the knowledge will remain safe even so – carried in and held by the next batch of arrivals.

And let us not forget the old. As their training begins to become less relevant and slip away, many seem to revisit the child's world with mature understanding and delight, often to the point of rapture. Again, Einstein's words are relevant: "The pursuit of truth and beauty is a sphere of activity in which we are permitted to remain children all our lives". To me, his words gracefully underline the need for those babies on the conference table.

6

Coming in from the cold
can be costly

"POETS", said Shelley – by which I take him to mean the great brotherhood of creative minds, including the scientists – "are the unacknowledged legislators of the world". Indeed, they see further, and earlier, than the rest of us. And they create a cradle of words, colours, sounds, or even scientific formulae, to hold the unfamiliar subtleties they find. In Shakespeare's words:

" ... as imagination bodies forth
The form of things unknown, the poet's pen
Turns them to shapes, and gives to aery nothing
A local habitation and a name".

Such people can travel in the endless worlds of which the sirens sing, and bring back with them some of the 'airy nothings' they encounter. This poetic journey is, of course, one of the many meanings of the story of Odysseus and the Sirens, in Homer's *Odyssey* – a story repeated in many forms, and in every culture.

From my own South African experience of the apartheid years, I have seen that without the work of the 'poets' and their soaring imaginations, as well as the creativity and sheer sense of shared humanity and wonder that they trigger in others, a society is truly brutalised. But I have only now really understood and framed for myself the astonishing paradox that the health and sanity of any society depends on its madmen.

By madmen I mean those whose vision soars beyond the box; for whom, in fact, there is no box; in whom normal everyday connections can dissolve on the instant and reveal something utterly different. Such people live on a knife edge – mad, but not mad. Their capacity is not given to all, and the price for it can be high. Free spirits returning from the metaphorical sphere often make crash-landings.

A study by Kay Redfield Jamison of the major English-language poets born between 1705 and 1805, for instance, found that six of the 35 poets were committed to lunatic asylums, two others committed suicide, and more than half showed evidence of mood disorders or psychotic symptoms. Subsequently she studied 47 living poets, writers and artists, all of whom had won major prizes or awards in their fields, and found that 28 per cent had received treatment for affective disorder, and a further 29 per cent had taken anti-depressants or lithium or been hospitalised – significantly more than found in the general population.

Daniel Nettle, in his fine book *Strong Imagination* (OUP, 2001), from which this research is drawn, shows that the knife-edge actually arises within our genes. The delusions of the mentally ill and the creations of the artist spring from a common source. Indeed the underlying cognitive make-up of healthy individuals in creative professions has been shown to have an overlapping profile with schizophrenics.

So it's a trade-off. It seems that the price for high art and creativity in the human species is often mental illness. Indeed, many of us will have met some of those unfortunate individuals who – whether artistically gifted or not – have strayed into the world of dreams and become lost there.

Nettle argues persuasively that humans have thought the function of their 'poets' so valuable that, as a species, they – we – have been prepared to live with the mental misery to which it is yoked. Otherwise the gene may well have been bred out, there being no obvious adaptive reason for retaining it. It seems we are prepared to pay the price – about 2 per cent of the population in all cultures – because a proportion of this percentage allow us, from time to time, to fly high on the wings of imagination and metaphor, rather than permanently suffocating on the ground.

Byron once said "we of the craft are all crazy" – but truly these 'madmen' are in some respects saner than the rest of us. Without the great creative works of our ancestors, and even the tolerance of eccentricity, we would have far fewer beacons to sustain and inspire us, particularly in hellish times. Sir Geoffrey Jackson, for example, former British Ambassador in Guatamala, who was kidnapped and kept isolated in a hole in the ground for eight months, said that one of the strongest elements in keeping him sane and stable throughout the ordeal was all the poetry he had memorised as a child.

Another example is that of Chiune Sugihara, a Japanese consul official in Lithuania, who in 1940 signed more than 2,000 visas for Jews hoping to escape the Nazi invasion, despite his government's direct orders not to do so. Bound by the strict codes of Japanese society, and knowing that flouting them brought shame on his family, something even stronger impelled him – a well-known image already lodged in his culture: "Even a hunter cannot kill a bird which flies to him for refuge". A single sentence framed by an unknown 'madman' centuries before saved all those lives.

Many earlier societies were coherent enough for their populations to share in their dreams, myths, stories, proverbs and adages. But our own society is too fragmented now; too big, and too ill-educated. Many of my clients under 40 read no books, know no poetry, see or make no art. Getting and spending, seeking advantage, consuming in comfort, being celebrated for nothing much … these often seem to be their highest aspirations. And of those who do read, many insist that reason and rationality are sovereign. They would take Goya's words, 'the sleep of reason produces monsters', at their face value, unaware that both metaphorically and in daily reality, 'monsters' also guard the gateway to the realms of the unknown.

It's as if we are living in a terrarium, nothing too terrible, nothing too outstanding, a ceiling over our heads, and the arts themselves, those building blocks of the imagination, largely scaled down to terrarium-size. Creative individuals tend to pour their talent into TV, films, advertising, blockbuster books and computer games, where the material rewards are great. And of course we are worried, because our children are addicted to them.

But an acquired taste is often a conquered repulsion, and an addiction may be a concealed allergy caused by faulty nutrition. So when a child's natural hunger for nutritious, time-tested stories – their real spaceships – has been diverted to the synthetic and second-best, what else could the result be?

The majority of us, lacking the poets' double-edged gene and lucky enough to be called 'sane', huddle in our cosy terrarium, nibbling our art-and-poetry-lite, and occasionally wondering if that is all there is. Yet all the while our madmen and giants and poets are out there in the cold, calling us, calling us… and fewer and fewer people can hear them. We should all get out more.

7

Aliens are among us already!

BELIEF TAKES many forms. Things we cannot know but consider safe bets, such as that the sun will rise tomorrow or (not quite such a good bet these days) that the ground will remain steady under our feet. Things we think we know, but which for the majority of us are really acts of faith, such as the fact that the earth rotates on its axis round the sun – which we probably believe for the same reasons ordinary people in Galileo's time believed the sun went round the earth: an authority figure said so.

There is religious belief, deeply and sincerely held by some, equally sincerely dismissed as nonsense by others. There are socially and culturally conditioned beliefs, which generation by generation are effectively inculcated into most of us; and then other more extreme ones, engineered within political or religious groups and cults. There are beliefs adhering to a single generation or locality, such as that held by many people under about 35, living in the southern part of Britain, that if they are not healthy, wealthy, beautiful and wise they had better see a therapist.

There are provisional beliefs, to help us get through each day, like the belief that what we are doing matters. There are beliefs we say we base on evidence, but often without personal experience of that evidence, or without knowing it may be illusory or insufficient. There are dangerous beliefs, such as those held by most humans to some extent, that 'we' are different from, and better than 'they'. And there are harmless beliefs which we can grow out of when we know a bit more – like Father Christmas or the tooth fairy.

The eminent Victorian scientist, explorer and polymath Sir Francis Galton once fixed his attention, experimentally, on a picture of Mr Punch, making believe it possessed divine attributes. He addressed it reverently "as possessing a mighty power to reward or punish the behaviour of men towards it" – and was surprised, he said, how very easy that was to do. He was amazed how quickly he developed, and "long retained", the same feelings that "a barbarian entertains towards his idols" – over a comic character which he was aware he'd deliberately *chosen* because it was so obviously unfitted to arouse veneration!

What he had also demonstrated, of course, is a truth that over time I have come to recognise in ever greater depth – that *whatever* we focus on amplifies and acquires meaning. And the more single-minded the focus, the deeper and more all-consuming that meaning seems to become, until very often it mutates into fixed and full-blown belief.

In other words, the prisoner who focuses only on the cell he's in will become an expert on, and derive 'meaning' from, every detail, weaving complex or crazy theories about (for instance) the condition and pattern of the cell's paint and plaster, or the precise location of a mouse's hole – while virtually forgetting that there is a wide world outside. A depressed person is similarly a prisoner; ruminating in ever increasing detail on every element of his predicament – for that is all he sees.

This pattern manifests in so many clients in my therapy practice that I've come to the conclusion that the human mind can be seen as host and prey to all sorts of parasitical beliefs – emotions or ideas which, because of prolonged interest in and focus on them, grow powerful enough to take over the mind they inhabit. Negligible though they may be in proportion to the resources of the consciousness they usurp, ultimately they will draw increasing energy from their host until the part is able to masquerade as the whole.

Medieval people regarded such parasitical aspects of the mind as foreign entities, creatures of the devil, and had an entire bestiary of such entities, including the Incubus and the Succubus, which would slide into a mind as it slept. The metaphor is exact: when the mind sleeps (even while seemingly awake) destructive beliefs can take hold. Using current terminology, we could say that alien entities are already among us – aliens we know, however, to be spawned and bred within our own psyches.

Anxiety, for example, or Rage, may walk about and flourish as creatures in their own right, drawing life from a host mind which, though full of experience, resources, and creativity, becomes drained of will or motive power. (This is why, of course, it is an axiom of good therapies to externalise such states of mind, so that individuals can see themselves as separate from these debilitating beliefs and emotions, and begin to take control again.)

In the therapy room I have seen such trivialities squatting within an individual's mind, rendering them apparently helpless: alien, erroneous beliefs affecting, even arresting, a whole life. I remember, for example, a woman who believed her life hopeless because of her tendency to blush. She saw everything through the distortions of this alien possession. "Even when I hear about someone going through hard times, even something as terrible as terminal illness", she said, "I still think 'but you've also got it easy – you've never needed to deal with my awful problem' ". And a highly intelligent young man absolutely believed that "until I sort my head out I'm not even going to try and do anything like study or work or meet people – what's the point, I'll only mess it up." That particular belief had kept him in life's waiting room for years. Similar if less all-consuming difficulties exist for us all, of course. We keep our aliens under control most of the time, but when they escape they create chaos.

One way to disarm a belief, in therapy or in education, is to challenge and test its reality. But outside the therapy room or classroom, in the rush of daily events, such challenges are not easy or, sometimes, even possible. In fact from our still comfortable vantage point in the West we see other parts of the world reeling under the alien weight of conflicting, all-consuming beliefs. These aliens are literally inhuman. They turn decent men, women, even children into fanatics and murderers.

We have a better chance at disabling these aliens when they come, as Shakespeare says, in 'single spies'. But when they make common cause with other minds hosting similar beliefs and morph into 'battalions', then I haven't the foggiest how the resulting muddle, chaos, or inhumanity can be prevented or limited.

But I do know that the intractable belief of the zealot or fanatic may often have begun as a small, wondering or innocent thought, before becoming focussed, magnified and hardened, untested, into an alien monstrosity. I know, too, that direct, head-to-head opposition not only accelerates the growth of such monsters in others but can also spark an alien mirror-image in ones own mind.

For whether harmless, lethal, or truly useful, and no matter how persuasive, belief is always a masquerade, blurring this crucial distinction – *belief is not the same as knowledge*. When this discrimination is made, and experienced and understood, the alien dematerialises on the instant – nothing palatable remains for it to feed on.

8

A limit to explanations

THERE'S a joke about a boy whose exhausted parents take him to a child psychologist. Their son has terrorised cat, dog, siblings and visitors, constantly trashed his room, and made everyone's life a misery. Even in the consulting room he's torn the books and ridden the rocking horse to destruction.

"We've done our best to be understanding", say the traumatised parents. "But we get nowhere. Is there anything you can do?"

The psychologist nods, sits the child down, crouches beside him and whispers in his ear. The boy's eyes widen, and from that moment on he is a model of good behaviour.

"Your therapy is truly wonderful", say the awed parents. "And so quick! What exactly happened?"

"I explained things to him", says the psychologist.

"What did you explain?"

"I explained that if he didn't shape up *immediately*, I'd find him wherever he was, and beat the shit out of him."

Jokes, as we know, can yield a harvest of understandings and still remain funny. And there are certainly many ways of explaining the insights here. Effectively showing someone that actions have consequences. The paradox of parents attempting psychological understanding while the psychologist plays the authoritarian parent. The outsider supplying a crucial ingredient missing at home. The value of shock when an individual is impervious to anything else. The recognition that the only possible solution to a problem may be uncomfortably politically incorrect. And so on. And as well as all this, the story also demonstrates both the uses and limits of explanation.

The pattern which drives us to seek explanations must surely be hard-wired in us. The core questions, 'Who am I?' 'Where do I come from?' 'Where am I going?' 'What am I for?' must have been asked, at least in childhood, by every human being on earth. We look for what lies underneath ("when did you two meet?", "how did we get into this mess?") to explain puzzles and confusions on the surface. This is the active template when we go to psychotherapist or doctor. And a known and labelled explanation of our symptoms is often a great relief, even when the diagnosis is unpleasant.

So strong is our need for explanation, in fact, that we will often change our perception to keep what we can't explain consistent with what we can. In the classic experiment on expectation, a red ace of spades (for instance) shown momentarily to a subject is simply perceived as black. Cognitive dissonance triggers whatever behaviour is needed to bring consistency back to the scene. Life must go on.

Indeed for explanations to do their work they need not even be true. There's an exercise I learned from clinical psychologist Michael Yapko which cheers depressed people up no end. To help gain some flexibility, a depressed person is asked to generate six alternative explanations for a distressing event. Say they have been short-changed at the supermarket. Their reaction might be: "I'm such a loser! The cashier saw me coming! Bad things always happen to me!" But other explanations might be: "her child's sick and she's preoccupied", "she's short-changing everyone", "it was a genuine mistake", and so on. The therapist can then point out that it's impossible to know which, if any, explanation is the true one, and suggests that the patient picks one that makes them feel OK rather than one that causes misery. When they do this – I see it again and again – they experience a real sense of liberation.

And if no satisfactory explanation can be found, phenomena are usually ignored and thereby rendered invisible. I remember the story of a friend from a far-off land, in Britain under cover. Though young, he had immense responsibilities back home, of which most people he knew here were unaware. One day he was sitting in his flat-share chatting with a bunch of friends, when one of them idly flipped open a suitcase and noticed a photograph of him on a parade ground taking a salute from hundreds of troops. "Oh ha ha!" said the friends. "Look at him in that funny uniform! What a joker!" And then simply resumed their conversation.

Primitive people's 'explanations' of the world they find themselves in are based on limited understanding, and we call their beliefs 'mere superstition'. But there is nothing 'mere' about it. Those explanations stabilise a chaotic world and enable individuals to get on with their lives. In this specific respect, modern science serves a similar function. Our knowledge, though considerably greater than that of the primitive, is still limited, and in any case most scientific 'discovery' is provisional – to be revised again and again. But each new finding is greeted, in the teeth of the evidence, as if we had at last found the truth.

In our own times cults offer a similar illusion of stability – by imprisoning their members within the explanations of a closed belief system. But such explanations are always spurious. Because – unlike primitive societies making their best bet at explaining what they saw around them – our society has access to better information than that which cults will be offering.

Even a non-explanation will provide relief, as long as it looks like an explanation. For instance, if we want a small favour from people we don't know, we are obviously more likely to get it if we explain why we want it. But in 1978 Langer et al went further. Experimenters tried jumping a queue in order to photocopy five pages. Most people in the queue – 94% – let them do so when given an explanation, but only 60 per cent agreed when given none. However, the experimenters then tried simply using the word 'because', adding nothing new: "I have five pages. May I use the photocopier because I have to make some copies?" And 93% agreed.

No wonder, then, that there are more than 60 synonyms for 'because' in my thesaurus, and hundreds of associated words. No wonder children invent wild and surreal explanations of what's going on around them – which they report with the utmost seriousness. No wonder rationalisation is a human industry. And no wonder the 'reframe' is such a powerful tool in psychotherapy.

And here's the nub of it. That which has no explanation makes us anxious – and anxiety paralyses. The mechanism which induces us to move again is explanation, whether true, or merely plausible, or wild rationalisation, or downright bluff. In a constantly changing environment, and particularly in disabling circumstances, explanations settle things. They give us a breathing space, steady the ground under our feet.

But explanation has its limits. Which is why, among other things, the ornate archaeological explanations arrived at in psychoanalysis seldom seem to produce much change. It seems to me that this is because explanation is not the same as experience. Having a 'reason', however, will make us relaxed enough to face and ultimately solve the next problem, and thereby take a step forward – towards the next explanation.

9

The man in the shiny
red plastic suit

IN RECENT years a multiracial group of South African actors
travelled the world with an exuberant production of the *Chester
Mystery Plays*, giving themselves totally to their enactment of the
Bible characters, lighting up the old stories with music, voice and
body, and rendering them inspiring, raunchy, energetic, moving
and funny.

And among the characters portrayed, none is more energetic and
raunchy than a man wearing a shiny red plastic suit and a salacious
grin, tongue thrusting in and out like a motorised dog-prick, hovering
round the edges of the action whenever greed or weakness is about
to surface. Just when the characters are wavering in a moment
of crisis, just when it dawns on them that it's possible not to do
the right or essential thing, there he is – not directly manipulating
anything himself, or needing to, but evoked seemingly by a climate
of confusion, doubt, fear, or sheer fatigue.

Though not religious myself, I began to ponder about that fallen
angel we call the devil. I realised I had no understanding at all of
whether there are forces of evil originating outside the terrestrial
environment. But I came up with a story which would, for ten
minutes or so, be one way of accounting for the devil's manifestation
within the human compass here on earth.

Perhaps, I thought, various versions of the man in the shiny red
suit had been generated within the world religions by the early
custodians of the human race, in order to help us deal with the
difficulties and temptations which swirl around in this beautiful and
corrosive world of ours. Those urges which arise in us seemingly
unbidden: 'Take the easy option.' 'Wish someone dead.' 'Steal
someone's property.'

And that kind of prompting, if followed, would have been
so wide of the mark that it would have generated, then as now,

paralysing feelings of powerlessness, grief and self-loathing for which these days we have a variety of specific psychological labels.

So was the devil created by those wise men for exactly the same reason that good therapists separate the core individual from the problem – because when overwhelmingly selfish, negative or destructive thoughts and impulses are externalised individuals discover that they can see things for what they are – and that they have, after all, choices, options and a measure of control?

That would mean that the devil can be understood, among other things, as a metaphor and dumping ground for every thought and impulse in the human mind and make-up which is unproductive, degrading, poisonous or wrong. And in the process what was 'inhuman' would be externalised, personified and defined. The definition even took into account the nature, degree, and gravity of these 'inhuman' impulses and energies by naming legions of imps, and lesser and greater demons, all the way down to the black and baleful Beast himself.

Projected out there in this way, the devil became an indispensable goad and prod, reminding us to think before we acted, to take care, to be restrained or forthright as appropriate, to be generous, to align ourselves with the biggest possible picture we were capable of apprehending. And if we couldn't see the whole picture, then to make our intentions as clean as possible, do our very best – and then learn from our mistakes.

In short, the man in the shiny red plastic suit within the various religions was an effective teacher, showing us what not to do, warning us to consider the consequences of our thoughts and actions, both on ourselves and on others.

But over time the accumulated build-up of apprehension about sin, evil and hell from the religious bureaucrats without, and the conditioning machinery within, must have so terrified us that like panicked animals we were no longer able to think, or learn, for ourselves.

Perhaps, my fantasy continued, the Old Testament story of Moses going up the mountain to receive a message from God to take to his people would have been at least partly about an attempt to free human beings from the constraints and fear of an externalised devil. The children of Israel had suffered and struggled and lost so many illusions and been through so many new experiences that they must have seemed ready for this step.

But when Moses comes down again, with a method of teaching the more inward understanding which can be found within the human mind, he sees the children of Israel, restraint thrown to the winds, worshipping a golden calf and behaving with a degree of licentiousness and lack of restraint not unlike that with which we're familiar in our own society today.

So Moses realises that in general the people are not yet ready to be their own guardians, and grimly returns to the mountain to carve out a set of ten external rules and prohibitions which will keep humanity safe until a subtler, more inward experience again becomes a possibility.

Perhaps, too, a similar pattern unfolded in our own era, when, with the growth of science, the devil's grip on our imagination began to loosen. Given the level of detachment a scientific approach engenders, and the fright and dread the concept of burning in hell had built up in us over the centuries, it again seemed an opportunity to return the responsibility to where it actually lay. External threats and promises could be replaced by internal perception and (to some extent) control.

But again, though the capacity is there in individuals, it may not yet be strong enough in the group, and the disappearance of the devil seems to have been taken by our own society to mean that evil itself no longer exists – except, perhaps, as a self-serving tabloid taunt. In effect we let go our primitive steering mechanism without replacing it with anything else, and cast ourselves adrift, like those early wanderers in the desert.

Mystics and theological scholars tend to talk about sin as 'missing the mark', or 'not being there'. Both phrases indicate that if we are really conscious within a situation then we can do nothing else but that which is required. Indeed in a seminal article on expectation (Great Expectations, J.Griffin, *Human Givens* Vol. 11 No. 1, 2004), Joe Griffin describes the mechanisms in the brain by which, if a clear intention is present, stale, habitual, mechanical or addictive responses can be removed from automatic, low-level processing and brought into the fresh air of volitional control and conscious decision – often with remarkable personal results.

Is it going too far to suggest that there are times when in place of 'addictive responses' we could substitute the words 'whatever we desire against our better judgement', be it cream cakes, our neighbour's spouse, falling in line with inhuman authority, or world-domination? For if the human mind were not equipped to learn how to escape from time to time from the loop of addictive or conditioned or even what used to be called sinful behaviour, then our ancestors could not have brought us this far, and the domain of the fallen angel in the shiny red plastic suit would be our entire and inexorable reality.

10

Being an insider
is no joke

A FEW YEARS ago a group of tribesmen from Papua New Guinea were brought to Britain by a TV company, to take a look at us.

On their first day they went on the London Eye. The Chief pointed to various buildings dominating the panorama. "What's that?" he asked, indicating St Paul's. His anthropologist host, seeking an understandable equivalent for 'cathedral', said "That's a God-house". The Chief pointed to the Gherkin. "And that?" "A money-house". And so on.

Back on the ground, the group were asked their impressions. The Chief said: "I see that you are people with very many money-houses and very few God-houses, and that all your money-houses are taller than your God-houses." In minutes, he had gleaned by observation a basic fact about our society. I doubt whether any words could now convince the Chief that our society loves God more than Mammon. Just by looking, he saw the truth for himself.

Within our own society too, uninvolved outsiders tend to see clearly what those working within the system miss. Here are some random examples, which no amount of insider argument can contradict. First, if meeting targets is really your primary (if unstated) purpose, then your stated purpose will fail. Second, it is extremely hazardous for private individuals to lend money they don't have, and the same goes for banks. Third, when a country surrenders its ability to feed and heat itself to other nations, it puts its future in peril.

However insiders – by which I mean our leaders and their equivalents at all levels, not excluding bureaucrats, who must frame policy, take decisions, and carry them out – don't see it that way. Vested interests, bias, preconception, the many details, plus their entanglement in the status quo, blur the bigger picture.

Few sane people would want to carry such an odious burden.

But the price to be paid for shunting the load onto those who are prepared to become our leaders and managers is to accept that for the above reasons and perhaps necessarily, they will be quite seriously disadvantaged, and sometimes even psychologically disturbed.

The unfortunate insiders compensate (as they must, to be effective) by taking themselves very seriously. When challenged they bluster, pull rank, become dismissive or very angry. Many are despotic or full of self-congratulation, and most are devoid of any real humour. They may have verbal wit, or the ability to wisecrack, but I can think of few in public life who seem able to laugh at themselves.

Self-mockery is essential.

However it seems to me that healthy laughter and self-mockery are essential for the deflation of pomposity and ego, and for self-criticism in individuals, communities or cultures. But this recourse is not really available to the powerful. When President Obama, for instance, publicly made himself the butt of his jokes, as he did early on in his presidency at a White House correspondents' dinner (for instance, he unambiguously mocked his own 'god-like' reputation) he was roundly criticised by many of his supporters, and even more of his opponents.

Indeed, I wonder if you can ever be top dog, and truly laugh at yourself, without it being taken by many people as a sign of weakness. Perhaps this is a liability of leadership. And perhaps this is why for many centuries, all over the world, people at the top employed others to do the mocking for them. The highest in the land, and not only kings, kept jesters, clowns, dwarves or professional Fools – entertainers with a license to needle and tacitly advise.

Through much of history, and all over the world, they seem to have taken to their work with zest. James VI of Scotland, for instance, used to be very lazy about reading things before signing them, until his jester, George Buchanan, tricked him into abdicating in favour of Buchanan himself – who became, for 15 days, technically the king. Queen Elizabeth I clearly welcomed her jester's taunts, for she is said to have chided him for not being sufficiently severe with her. And in Iran in the 19th century, I am told, the autocratic Shah Nasrredin terrified his courtiers, but never his jester. When, for instance, the Shah asked whether there was, as he'd heard, a food shortage, the jester replied: "Well I see Your Majesty is eating only five times a day."

Jesters probably got away with it because most of the time they were amusing and entertaining, and could fill the court with laughter. That gave them license to speak freely on occasions when the rest of the court dared not. For instance, in 1340, when the English destroyed the French fleet at the Battle of Sluys, the nervous courtiers left it to Phillippe VI's jester to break the news. "I have heard", he told the king, "that the English sailors don't even have the guts to jump into the water like our brave French".

As the lowliest member of the court the Fool, like all outsiders, was genuinely uninvolved. He could express the very things that would send a well-born adviser to the block. His detached mental posture is wonderfully summed up by Feste, the jester in Shakespeare's *Twelfth Night*, when he says: "Nay, I am for all waters". And though the insults might sting, they were accompanied by shrewd and very human understanding, which probably accounts for the real affection between most Kings and their Fools. If a jester could talk the king out of harming an innocent citizen, it would not only save the victim from injustice, but also save the king from himself.

The jester has long gone from the courts and corridors of power, but in fact he still exists: sharp, funny, and courageous; clear-sighted, mocking and critical; usually well-educated now – and self-employed. We encounter him or her on radio or TV, and through the contents of Private Eye. And what the best of them do is beyond price.

Yet even so, the insiders, our leaders, simply laugh along with the rest of us! They seem impervious to the well-placed shafts and barbs – perhaps because the comments are not from their personal jester. They are not paying him, so have no investment in taking the mockery to heart

As a remedy, then, should Parliament employ a jester of its own? There are brilliant contenders around. But of course there's a catch. We taxpayers would end up footing the bill – and then, in a sense, the joke would be on us.

11

It came off in me 'and Guv!

A WIFE deliberately goads her husband beyond breaking point, then blames him for his rage. An obstetrician does an unnecessary Caesarian section, rather than risk blame should a normal delivery go wrong. An oil tanker breaks up, and rather than co-operate to contain the spill, an unseemly wrangle between Britain and Spain breaks out about whose fault it is.

Anthropologists divide societies into 'guilt cultures' and 'shame cultures', but ours has escalated into a culture of constant blame – and to hell with whoever we might affect in the process. Excuses and accusations trip instinctively off the tongue: "It's not my fault, Guv. It came off in me 'and". Or – "It wasn't me, Squire – it was him!" As that brilliant satirist Dr Theodore Dalrymple has written: "Man is born immortal, yet everywhere he dies – and it's always somebody's fault."

Sometimes, blame reaches surreal heights. There's a centuries old traditional tale about this, but there is also an actual case on record in America – when a burglar fell through the badly tiled roof of a house, broke his leg and successfully sued the house owner. At other times, blame lies at the heart of catastrophe. Indeed we see every day how the most sublime and exceptional of men, who lived many centuries ago, are today often held personally responsible and bitterly blamed for the terror which madmen perpetrate in their name.

Blame also generates excitement – and like any other state of high arousal, as we know, excitement overrides clarity and rationality and allows us to think only in the crudest, black-and-white terms. We're familiar with this in the media – in the frantic pursuit of excitement, they daily hunt down, exaggerate and assign blame, broadcasting faults (accurate or not) which might not otherwise have been much noted, and glorying in each head that rolls and reputation that topples.

But then, it seems that no human culture is immune from blame. For example in the third century BC Buddhist text, the Dhammapada, we find: "This is an old saying, Atula, it is not a saying of today: 'They blame the man who is silent, they blame the man who speaks too much, and they blame the man who speaks too little.' No man can escape blame in this world."

Blame, in fact, is part of our nature – stemming, I think, from our animal side, which operates by pecking order and hierarchy. The army, the health and social services, almost every political and commercial organisation and nearly every social group, all are hierarchies playing a game of human snakes and ladders, using praise and blame, reward and punishment, as their method of control.

This generates constant tension. We must keep watching our backs and asking ourselves whether we measure up, and when we do something wrong the most reliable way to survive is to pass the buck, fast. Indeed, perhaps pointing the finger is our national pastime because we know that our performance often leaves something to be desired, and in the hierarchical world of (often) random blame, we could easily be found guilty of *something*.

But we are more than animal, and therefore torn. Our biology compels us to seek the comfort and safety of the hierarchy and the herd, while our humanity tells us that blame is neither ethically justified nor practically useful. So what can we do, caught in this insoluble dilemma? If we know that it is impossible to rid ourselves completely of this ancient template, can we ever side-step the finger-pointing or the guarding of our status?

To some extent, I think we can. As engineers do. They work in groups which are not very hierarchical, because if they are going to get their planes to fly or their software to work then solving problems is more important than dodging blame. Whatever the project, they know how much can and probably will misfire or fail along the way. They know that it doesn't matter who made the mistake, what matters is what can be learned from it. And they also know that solutions are normally found by the people on the ground, and that absolutely anyone might supply a crucial 'wheeze' or piece of knowledge. Mistakes, to engineers, are not personal. They are feedback.

It is so simple, really. Remove the emotional heat from mistakes, treat them as useful, and we can progress. Our language itself contains the metaphor. We 'grasp the nettle' – because if we do, then it can provide us with nutrition instead of stinging us, which it inevitably will do if we simply brush past it.

So why do we find this so hard?

Well, there's the over-arching biological impulse towards hierarchy. There's the fact that we are overpopulated and constantly jockeying for position. There's the feeling of being out of control as social change and technological complexities quicken around us. There's the peculiarity in our culture, pointed out by Lionel Trilling, himself a critic, that we honour the act of blaming, taking it as the sign of virtue and intellect. And crucially, there's the helplessness and dependence we feel because we are no longer encouraged to take responsibility for ourselves.

This dependence is intensified by a consumer society which prefers us to be sheep; to refer outwards; to think that what we want and absolutely must possess is what everyone else apparently wants and must possess – whatever is fashionable, whether in clothes or behaviour or ideas. And if we don't get these things, we are further led to think, there must be something wrong, and we should look for who or what to blame. This feeling of being wronged can in many cases lead straight to the therapy room. (And what was psychoanalysis but an ingenious way of shifting the blame onto the past, and those who could not answer back?)

People who come to therapy blame all manner of things for their difficulties, but mostly they blame themselves. Yet all that may be wrong is that these individuals actually believe the external, consumerist view of what life should look like. They have tried hard to deny their needs, restyle their minds, even reshape their bodies, in an effort to seem like everyone else, and it isn't working. For them, esteem and success are measured only in terms of how others see them and whether these others will 'buy' what they see.

For instance a beautiful young girl, slender and well-proportioned, and more importantly, with a gentle and caring nature, recently informed me that she desperately wanted a breast reduction. Why? "Well men don't like girls with big chests", she said mechanically, which told me how often she had blamed her breasts for her loneliness. "Would you be interested in a man who could only love you if you had the right bra size? Would *you* want *him*?" "No", she said with surprise, breaking out of the consumer trance on the instant.

Clearly the perfection she craved when she looked outward bore no resemblance to what she wanted when she looked within. She could have rid herself of her mistaken assumption years ago, by changing the direction of her gaze and coming to see mistakes, problems, faults and needs as guides and teachers, to be observed calmly, and welcomed rather than avoided. It is a truism because it is true that if you don't learn from your mistakes you are condemned to repeat them.

Perfectionism has many roots, and the desire to keep or improve status in the pecking order is one of them. But we live in an unstable world, buffeted by forces we don't understand or even perceive. Nature is 'red in tooth and claw', the atmosphere is corrosive, entropy rules. Until our story is done, there is no such thing as completion or closure. All is process. Under such circumstances, to look for people to blame, and to insist on being blameless oneself, is to stall one's life.

Doing something well is always the result of a series of corrected mistakes. Every child learns to stand by falling down. Walking itself is controlled falling. Every aircraft landing is a controlled crash. Indeed, life can be seen as something like a tightrope walk with a long balancing pole. When we tip too far one way or the other, we register the feedback and use the balancing pole to steady us, so we may continue forward.

And when we realise that being on the high wire is actually our daily condition, then responsiveness is all and blame becomes irrelevant.

12

Knowing where
you belong

THE NEED to belong has been identified as a 'human given'. But belong to what, exactly? This question threads through an absorbing memoir I've just read: *My Innocent Absence*, by Miriam Frank, highly respected for her work in anaesthetics, and now, in her retirement, a writer and translator.

Frank is Jewish, born in Spain during the civil war to a single mother who has fled Germany. Her Lithuanian-born father is mostly absent, and lives much of the time in America. By the time she is 12 she and her mother have run from two wars and lived on three continents. So as a child she was already an outsider. She writes of life in North Africa, Spain and France, of escaping with her mother by boat to Portugal when she was five, then on to Mexico for several years, and then to New Zealand, where she finishes her education and trains as a doctor. She has spent time in Germany and Argentina, has lived in Israel, Italy, and Britain (now her home), and has acquired the languages of her many host countries. So she can appear to fit in more or less anywhere. Her masterful use of English in her elegantly told, beautifully observed memoir makes this fit clear: she is up there with the best.

Unsurprisingly, however, wherever she lives, she feels herself 'different', even in very small ways, as a poignant example illustrates. Newly arrived in New Zealand, and finding it painfully narrow-minded, twelve-year-old Miriam is told by her German aunt that she may not have breakfast until she changes out of the pretty red dress, unremarkable in Mexico, that she had put on that morning. "Why?" asks the baffled child. "We do not wear red in New Zealand", she is told implacably. "Put on a pastel colour." She goes upstairs, misses the breakfast, and cries her heart out.

Belonging obviously implies a barrier, between an 'us', and ... not so much a 'them' as a variegated soup of 'not us'. If balanced, this is healthy. Common interest groups, social, professional, and so on, nourish us and are useful. National pride within bounds is beneficial too. But we know only too well the tragic consequences, the devastations of holocaust and genocide, once that pride escalates into heartless hatred of others.

I have heard people shrug and say 'well, that's human nature'. But there's nothing human about it. It's pre-human. It's what animals do. They kill or shun others of their ilk who are wounded, or in some way don't fit. I have watched it time and again with animal herds in the African bush. It is the law of the jungle, not the path of humanity.

'Otherness' is identified within the social consensus nearer home too, and the cost of it may last a lifetime. I am old enough myself to remember a time when the 'mad' were thought so alien that they were locked out of sight and seldom mentioned. (Indeed, Miriam Frank's vivid description of psychiatric wards she worked in as a student evokes a sense of sheer hell.) I remember, too, a time when cancer was mentioned only in whispers, and *never* to those who had it. In those days, too, most unmarried pregnant women had their babies removed at birth, and some of those mothers were hidden in mental hospitals for years. Again, not too long ago, the otherness of homosexuality risked prosecution and prison. The prodigious brilliance and promise of Alan Turing was sacrificed to this, as was the dazzling talent of Oscar Wilde.

And lo! All this has gone away!

Except that it hasn't gone away. The focus on 'otherness' has simply moved. These days there is little shame in mental illness, nor in the formerly unspeakable 'Big C'. Is that, I wonder, because we have now become so concentrated on our own physical and mental health? And did this intense interest begin when we lost religion? As hopes of a next world faded, for many, into disbelief, did we start to focus on keeping ourselves physically and mentally fit and safe, in order to survive as long and comfortably in *this* world as possible?

It seems that we humans are only able to manage a limited amount of sanity, and shift our madness, prejudice and distaste for otherness from one place to another. But the *proportion* of the conformist 'need to belong' seems to remain constant. These days, for instance, we're all trying to be 'individual' and 'distinctive', not noticing that a visitor from Mars wouldn't actually be able to tell the difference between us. Perhaps the herd behaviour I mentioned earlier is not far from the truth.

Fortunately, it seems that for every act of brutality, ignorance, hostility and distaste between one group of us and another, there are, though in smaller numbers, always humane attempts by some people, regardless of allegiances, to be of genuine help.

Miriam Frank is one of these. In spite of everything that happens to her, including a tumultuous and difficult marriage, she remains almost child-like in her openness and generosity, and in the freshness of the questions she asks herself. Having seen so much violence and destruction she decides, very young, to become a doctor, as a way to help humanity, not damage it. And in her long search for where she might belong, she chooses at one point to live in Israel, thinking after a while that she's found the answer at last. But that too wears out. There are so many transgressions against otherness there that in the end she can't ignore them.

When, over many years, all has been said and done, this permanent outsider comes to realise that the only 'belonging' that makes sense is to become a fully paid up member of the human race. Easy to say, hard to come to, but once accepted, many things hidden from those living within narrower boundaries may be seen and understood. It seems to me that attempting to belong to the community of humans has built-in problems of its own, but in the end nothing less is worth the attempt. An illuminating saying from *The Gulistan* (*Rose Garden*) by Sheikh Saadi of Shiraz in the 13th century, translated and passed on to me by my husband David Pendlebury, contains the essence of this and expresses it beautifully: 'Wherever the seeker lays his head at night is his palace'.

13

The meaning is not always the message

MY CHARMING client L says she knows that she and M, a good friend whose love she yearns for but who in fact is marrying another, are 'meant' for each other because coincidences constantly bubble up between them. The latest is that street and house numbers of the new flat the local Council has just given her, together form his birth date, and the house itself turns out to be where he parks his car on his way to work.

I tell her, truthfully, that our local Council assigns different numbers to each wheelie-bin, and the six-digit registration number on the lid of ours comprise the numbers of my husband's birthday. By her reckoning, would that mean that somehow he should leave me and marry the wheelie bin, or that his life is garbage?

When phenomena are little understood it's a very human tendency to see their meaning, as my client has done, in terms of their impact on us – and as a friend once did when a smallish earthquake shook the ground beneath his feet as he started to give a lecture. In the absence of other information, for a few moments he interpreted the shaking as meaning he was having a heart attack.

But we can go very wide of the mark when we 'interpret' coincidences in this personal way, as if they were our dreams. They may in fact simply point to a different pattern from the one we normally perceive. A coincidence itself showed me this. As I walked down an unfamiliar street one afternoon, many years ago, I saw a couple with a small child on the far pavement, and a man coming towards them from the other direction. Two cars, one with a passenger, were travelling down the road in different directions. And on the nearside pavement three people, of whom I was one, were passing each other. For a split-second cars and people all coincided – you could have drawn a line from pavement to pavement which would have gone through us all.

But that moment could have been seen as a coincidence only by me – because I knew every single one of those other nine people: pedestrians, drivers, passenger. They had arrived there for a split-second from quite unrelated areas of my life, and as far as I am aware wouldn't have known each other. You'd be hard-pushed to find personal significance in that fleeting moment.

Arthur Koestler called coincidences "the puns of destiny", but I think they are more like a curtain momentarily drawn aside, or a paving stone which has been prised up, revealing the pipes and wiring for electricity, gas, phone and so on, which until that moment we've been walking over unawares. We constantly use these amenities unthinkingly, then suddenly our attention is focussed on their network of transmission. The analogy is imprecise, but throws light both on how we misconstrue, as we try to make sense of the slice of the pattern we see, and also on how interconnected everything is: the energies themselves, the pipes and wires that carry them, the multitude who benefit from them, the brilliant thinkers who discovered and harnessed them, those on whose shoulders they stood to do so, those who currently maintain them, and so on, endlessly, all knitted together – and impersonal.

Coincidences fascinate, I think, because like fairytales they signal something "more" and start us wondering about possibilities beyond those we normally account for. Some are extraordinary – like the strange and well-known parallels between the assassinations of Presidents Kennedy and Lincoln. We are all familiar with such odd conjunctions in our own lives, and here is one of mine. When my friend Laurens told me he was going to India I thought he'd enjoy meeting my friend Maggi, who lived there. Though I hadn't seen her since we were nine we both felt ourselves as close as sisters, and were regularly, though not frequently, in touch, and still are. I tore a page from a notebook and scribbled a letter introducing her to Laurens.

Weeks later he wrote saying he hadn't travelled as far south as Maggi lived and was leaving India in two days, so wouldn't be able to see her. But the next day a series of coincidences sent him unexpectedly to Madras, while another set of coincidences carried Maggi there, most unwillingly. She found herself lunching in a hotel she'd sworn never to set foot in again – and Laurens was at the next table. Because his face seemed familiar she thought she must know him (actually she'd seen his picture on book jackets: he was a well-known writer) and so she asked him if they'd perhaps met. He said he thought not, but invited her to join him, and as she moved tables she introduced herself. "Oh!" said Laurens when he heard my name "I have a letter for you in my pocket". She read it and smiled: "I wondered why I packed two saris for an overnight trip. One is obviously for Pat."

Statistics, of course, dismisses the oddness of anecdotes like this by demonstrating that "unusual" patterns are far more commonplace than we imagine. Indeed I've read a superb satirical essay entitled "Scientific Proof of My Divinity" by mathematician Rob Berry, in which he produces a whopping amount of "unusual instances" of "the holy number 7" in his life to "prove with mathematical certainty .... that I myself am God." The whole exercise has an awful, spurious, plausibility.

But in spite of statistics I think that there are times when we are somehow "tuned in", when a facet of the wider coincidence can also be personally helpful. There's the well-known phenomenon of the Library Angel, which we've probably all experienced – when (for instance) the very book we need and couldn't find is plonked down in front of us by the person returning it, or when we pull a book at random from an unlikely shelf, open it any-old-where, and find the page contains precisely the information we've been searching for.

Indeed I have a fancy that individuals exist who are so consistently "tuned in" that they walk step by step through a constant shifting field of coincidences, at each moment seeing (should they choose to) the way I saw, for a fleeting second, that line in a street through the heart of ten people. I wonder if we are all doing this more often than we realise – and just occasionally we see it.

14

Healthy curiosity is
precisely that...

FOLLOWING his outstanding contribution to the development of the atom bomb in World War II, Richard Feynman became Professor of Theoretical Physics at Cornell University. At 27, he was already unsurpassed in his field, and increasingly tempting job offers from other universities kept landing regularly on his desk.

Unsurprisingly, in the heat of all the accumulating expectation, his inspiration evaporated, so much so that he feared he was "burned out". No research idea even began to spark his interest. What could be important or valuable enough to justify the astronomical money on offer? The last straw came when Princeton University offered him a better position than even Einstein had had there.

But then a single thought set him free. He realised that attempting to live up to others' preconceptions was absurd, and he had no responsibility to deliver the impossible. Physics had once been fun rather than work, because he had simply been following where curiosity led him. Now, he decided, he would make physics fun again, do only what he felt like doing, and to hell with "importance".

Within days he was watching someone fooling about in the cafeteria, throwing a spinning plate in the air. He saw the whole plate wobble and the central Cornell medallion at its centre spinning round, and he started scribbling equations working out the relationship between wobble and spin. Elated, he told his findings to a colleague, who wondered why he was bothering with something so trivial.

Feynman wasn't discouraged. He'd already decided 'importance' was unimportant. "It was like uncorking a bottle," he wrote later. "Everything flowed out effortlessly.... There was no importance to what I was doing, but ultimately there was. The diagrams and the whole business that I got the Nobel Prize for came from that piddling around with the wobbling plate."

Curiosity, which so charms and allures us, is one of mankind's greatest gifts – we couldn't even have come down from the trees without it. It is the power which drives genius. Leonardo da Vinci constantly questioned everyone he met, with intensity and focus, to find out what they knew and how things worked. Feynman was exuberantly interested in everything – from gambling to safe-cracking to dreaming to languages to practical jokes to playing the bongos. Though he saw himself as naïve and one-sided, his naïveté was more like the untrammelled astonishment of a child with endless worlds to explore.

In childhood, curiosity burns like a flame. Most people probably remember extraordinary things they explored and understood in their youth. Those who do not surrender this birthright of curiosity to coercion or convention seem to have an extra dimension in their lives. It comes as no surprise that many inventions, such as the telescope and microscope, had their birth as toys. Or that people who, like Leonardo and Feynman, retain their childlike wonder, are usually blessed with fruitful lives and many friends. As Dr Johnson observed, the distinguishing mark of a "generous and elevated mind" is an "eminent degree of curiosity".

Historian G.M. Trevelyan saw disinterested curiosity as "the life-blood of real civilisation" – an observation so self-evident that we take it for granted. Could this be partly why there's comparatively little focus on curiosity in research? Only sporadic studies can be found over the last century, often as a minor theme in general research on motivation. However motivation is not the same as pure curiosity.

Motivation suggests an axe to grind, or an end to be gained. Human curiosity is neutral. Its aim, even when intense, is simply to learn and understand – a mental posture markedly different from both inquisitiveness and nerdishness. Where the nerd obsessively collects information, the curious individual is lit by the sheer open-minded joy in finding things out. And while curiosity is yoked to imagination and creativity, inquisitiveness can actually be dangerous because it is mindless, frequently prurient, and unduly reckless. Inquisitiveness, I contend, not curiosity, is what really killed the cat.

But lack of curiosity will starve the cat, because without it the light of the mind is quenched. Even Feynman's virtually inexhaustible mind was worn away by the pressure of those escalating job offers. And in depressed or anxious people we see the extreme – individuals so trapped within the darkness of their negative introspections that the world is defined by their difficulties. Nothing else exists, so nothing else can interest them. But when I hear a client at the end of therapy saying in wonder, as many do, often using identical words, "nothing has changed but everything is different now", I know their minds are freed, bright again with healthy curiosity.

Everything has its price. Curiosity's cost is the confusion and discomfort of relinquishing current understanding in favour of what is still unknown. Indeed, this pattern exists in certain myths and stories. The curiosity of Bluebeard's wife, for instance, leads her to discover behind a locked, forbidden door the corpses of her husband's former wives. The shocking revelation frees her to escape what would have been her destruction, and move on to a new life and new husband who truly loves her.

In the Bible it is Eve's curiosity that propels mankind out of the Garden of Eden, from a state of innocence into a growing consciousness of good and evil. And Pandora too (who in Greek mythology was – like Eve – the first mortal woman on earth) opens a forbidden box and releases evil into a formerly innocent world. Only Hope, curiosity's ally, remains – to see humanity through.

One thing I see in these stories is human beings evolving from a protected state of innocence to sink or swim in the dangerous and perplexing chaos of existence. And implicitly, that the return to equilibrium will be achieved by individuals consciously learning to find their way through it – no longer innocent and dependent but with an autonomy born of experience.

One could even wonder whether it's precisely the curiosity of these female characters that enables this process to unfold. Why else would their attention be constantly brought back to the tantalising prohibition – forbidden apple, sealed box, locked door – until it can no longer be resisted?

Curiosity, in fact, is always tempting us to go beyond the locked door. It disregards labels, is indifferent to the status quo, and finds ideas of status itself irrelevant or comical, as in the end Feynman found all those escalating job offers. He once said: "The prize is in the pleasure of finding the thing out, the kick is in the discovery

... those are the real things. Honours are unreal to me." In fact, in 1965, when he was woken by a phone call at 3 a.m. and told he had just won the Nobel Prize, and did he have any questions, he simply asked, I imagine with genuine curiosity: "Why couldn't you wait until morning?"

15

Lessons from
the long view

THE LACK OF the long view is everywhere these days. Instant gratification is an almost conventional requirement, while the past is a blurred irrelevance. Significant numbers of children think Hitler was British Prime Minister in World War II and that Oliver Cromwell fought in the Battle of Hastings in 1066 – an idea they will no doubt carry into adulthood.

The other day I heard, not for the first time, a young woman wonder how people got through World War II without benefit of counselling. Recently, also, a colleague was savouring how far psychotherapy had come since it began. "When would you say it did begin?" I asked. "Freud", he said, surprised at the question. "And before him?" "Well, you know," he said. "Horror. Bedlam. Snake-pits. That sort of thing …" How unlike our own enlightened times, when the mentally ill can at times be helpless and homeless and wandering the streets.

I probably shouldn't have been surprised. My colleague's words represent a widely held cultural assumption. Before Freud, the abyss – and aren't we lucky we escaped? In my own psychotherapy training, Freud was presented as the first in a series of orderly, evolving steps which brought us to our present elevated state of understanding. But in fact human nature hasn't changed over the centuries, and there's plenty of evidence that people have helped each other through difficulties ever since language emerged and myth and stories were born. From the moment, in fact, that anyone could feel, and tell a friend, that they knew the gods had it in for them.

During my training, too, I kept wondering why psychotherapy had to be so complicated, so lengthy, so systematic and so pessimistic. Had it always been like that? After all, Freud himself, though determined to be part of the scientific establishment, had in fact inherited – and drawn upon – the rich tradition of Jewish mysticism.

Indeed, when you look around you find psychotherapy's equivalents practised over centuries by priests, sages, elders, 'witches'. And also by ordinary people, no doubt, with their heads properly screwed on.

Years ago I was on an Italian campsite one midnight when someone ran amok. He was bellowing like a bull and charging the tents, bringing them down, one after another, as terrified people in their night-clothes fled out of harm's way. Someone rang the police; another actually called a friend in London to ask his advice. Many cowered and hid until, still bellowing, he was carried away in a strait jacket.

But I also have a contrasting memory – of a black man similarly running amok in a South African factory. With affectionate good humour his co-workers caught him, and sat on him, but with affection, laughing and joking, until the fit passed. These people may have been oppressed for close on three centuries, but they had been tempered by a wider range of experience than we, in our comfortable society, know anything about.

We congratulate ourselves, too, that we are learning to cut treatment times. But brief therapy isn't new. In the eleventh century, for example, a young woman suffering paralysis of the arms was brought to the physician Ibn Sina. He invited his associates to watch as he lifted the girl's veil. Then noting her deep blush, he gripped her skirt and raised it, slowly, higher and higher. The 'paralysed' arms soon moved to shake off his hand and pull her skirt down. Ibn Sina used the power of her modesty to heal her. (We'd take longer – or risk being charged with sexual harrassment.)

This type of simplicity born of accurate perception has always been what makes therapists outstanding, whenever they have lived. In the twentieth century Milton Erickson never narrowed his viewpoint or limited treatment options by aligning himself with systems or theories. In fact he once showed a student the trees lining the road outside his house, all bending south with the wind, and prompted him to notice that one was leaning towards the north. There are always exceptions. If you keep repeating what worked before, the work will not stay true. Therapy should be an art, even in our mechanical age. Systematisation stultifies.

Nor should we cling with superstitious deference to 'scientific' explanations – though we can respect the real meaning of that word:

knowing. Early last century Alfred Adler, asked by disappointed students why he no longer wrote in a 'scientific' way, replied with a smile that it had taken him most of his life to learn to write like a Jewish Granny. Such a posture precludes jargon – another obstacle noted in earlier times. In the fifteenth century, for example, the great Sufi poet Jami, when asked why he so seldom used technical terms, said: "Our aim is to have direct perception of the truth – not talk cleverly about it".

We have sophisticated descriptions of mental disturbance today, and know what goes on in the brain at a chemical or cellular level, but our treatment of mental disturbance may sometimes be no better than, sometimes not as good as, our predecessors. Tribal elders, for example, would put an initiation group through a series of unfamiliar, challenging and occasionally risky experiences which would induce them to reach for qualities and capacities they didn't even know they had, qualities essential to growth and maturation. In my own work I often feel I am trying inadequately to replace, within the constraints of our comfortable society, the work that in former cultures the initiation experience took care of.

The Old Testament prophet in *Ecclesiastes* affirms there's nothing new under the sun – even then, in the deep mists of history! Well before Christianity, Hippocrates recorded the psychological characteristics of cancer sufferers. And through the centuries you find references to the brain's hemispheric function. In the eighteenth century, for example, the German mathematician and natural scientist Lichtenberg wrote: "Whenever he was required to use his reason, he felt like someone who had always used his right hand, but was now required to do something with his left." In our terms for our times, we reformulate what others have known.

So three questions from my training days – does psychotherapy have to be complicated, systematic, and lengthy, are answered by taking the long view. As can the fourth: must it be pessimistic? Well, we live in a pessimistic society, and unless we look beyond its boundaries that pessimism will inevitably contaminate therapy.

In his book *Man, Beast and Zombie* (Orion Publishing Company 2002), neurophysiologist Kenan Malik clearly showed that science has limitations. And that by not noticing these, we are in the depressing position of adopting scientific postures when they are inappropriate, and seeing ourselves as nothing more than animals or machines. With so low a ceiling, no wonder we have lost hope and aspiration. In the words of Goethe: "He who cannot draw on 3,000 years of history is living from hand to mouth."

16

Round and round
and back again

IN ONE OF James Thurber's comic fables for our time, the 'moral' of a tale about an incompetent and gullible bear turns out to be: "You might as well fall flat on your face as lean over too far backward."

Like all the best humorists, he *wasn't* fooling. His 'moral' applies all over the place. For example, you might as well be trapped by too much emotion as hindered by too little feeling. In both states the bigger picture remains unseen, so we address our energies to mere fragments of it. In other words, while the house is burning, we are either in the corner of the garden diligently pulling out selected weeds, or else we are frantically berating the fire raisers, most often from a safe distance – which is about as effective as yelling abuse at someone on the radio.

Out at the extremes, there are tragic examples of young people inflated by ideas of heroism and ultimate service, or aflame with anger or frustration, while colder others, eyes fixed on their 'targets', feel little for the young lives they will 'sacrifice', as they manipulate their feelings and send them (along with many innocent others) to their deaths.

Climate change, too, produces the same phenomenon, and consequently nothing very effective gets done. On the one hand, many of us are paralysed, by fear perhaps, or a feeling of powerlessness, while others in a position to do so generate a blitzkrieg of uncoordinated solutions focussed on miniscule bits of the big picture. Eureka, a solution! Offset your carbon footprint! Make people pay for the garbage they generate (and inherit from the packagers)! A little way down the line, arising from the mess these 'solutions' themselves generate, our so-called public servants will spawn a new blitzkrieg of 'solutions' and strenuously apply them. And we will be trapped in the process, becoming servants of the very people who are supposed to be serving us.

The above are extreme situations, of course, but the pattern is also at work nearer home. Indeed it can be found inside our own minds. But in the world outside, the NHS is a good place to see it. Take, for example, the matter of 'targets'. I understand that patients with suspected cancer must now, quite rightly, be seen in the NHS within two weeks. But what is happening, so more than one doctor has told me, is that agitated, hysterical patients are whisked through, very often on false suspicions of life-threatening illness, while those who are more reticent and accepting, that is to say less emotional, but really do have cancer, may remain on the waiting list for months.

We're also told that waiting lists in hospitals have been greatly reduced. But in part that may be because appointments are often given to people known to be going on holiday, or are subsequently deferred well beyond the period the doctor has requested. In my case this year, the consultant asked to see me again in three months, but the appointment date the management sent me has turned it into six.

Both the above instances exemplify Alfred Korzybski's powerful words: "the map is not the territory". That is true even of the best maps, but here there is a virtual *abyss* between what the tick-boxes say and the territory. It is a fundamental mismatch, which will finally have to be acknowledged, and in the end usually is. Then surveys, commissions, enquiries and reviews will be announced. They will take time, discussions of the recommendations will take more time, and so it will go, till the next set of solutions. After that, as in the film *Groundhog Day*, the cycle will be repeated, round and round in circles yet again, until perhaps we learn.

But why must we try things out one at a time? When Jews study Talmud, I understand that one of their methods (and I assume all traditions have a similar exercise) is the technique of *pilpul* — a search for *every* meaning or explanation of a text that can be found. On the one hand, it could be this, on the other hand that, on the third hand the other ... and so on, all the way round the issue, seeing it in dozens of ways, as many as conceivable, in fact. And then, I surmise, having found all potential explanations, and exhausted all feasible perspectives, it becomes possible to go beyond them all, to a deeper understanding, a wordless altered perception, and perhaps a real step forward.

The difference between this approach and our own situation is a crucial one. No intention exists in our society to search for real understanding. What is required instead is 'performance' – that is to say, the appearance of things. And so we see ideas, policies, fashions, come and go, rise and fall, gallop the course and retire, and then return – refreshed with different names or a slightly altered orientation, having been dreamed up all over again, without any reference to the shortcomings that were encountered the first time round, or any understanding of how the previous expedients disappeared.

Yet without that bigger picture, past knowledge, and all the effort which went into achieving it, goes down the drain and is wasted, as in the story about the exhausted man and the servant. Whether the tale is true or not, the metaphor is exact, and many of us have experienced it in one form or another:

A noted historian and theologian, commissioned by a Historical Society in Amsterdam to translate the *Dead Sea Scrolls* into simple language, was due to deliver his manuscript the following day. He had barely slept in the final weeks, battling to finish his huge work on time.

Very close to the deadline, his wife persuaded her exhausted husband to have a quick sandwich and a short nap. "You can sort out the last few details when you wake," she said.

Two hours later he returned to his desk, refreshed and alert – and found no sign of either his manuscript or his capacious notes.

"What happened to my papers?" he yelled at his wife. "I don't know," she said. "No one has been in your study except the servant – I asked her to tidy up a bit while you slept." The servant was summoned. "What have you done with my papers?" ranted the author, almost incoherent with anxiety.

"Don't worry Sir," said the servant. "I only burned the papers that were already written on. You'll find the nice clean sheets in your desk drawer."

17

Just how many books
do we need?

THE OTHER day I read two aphorisms, both many centuries old, that flew like darts into my mind (which must have been open at the time) and lodged there.

The first said: "Do not regret the past and do not worry about the future." The second said in effect: "When we speak, we take care not to make a mistake in grammar. How is it we take no similar care with our actions?"

Each one struck like a blow. For a moment I saw the distance I could travel with either saying – given, that is, effort, work, and time. If I was up to it, each could powerfully change the way I perceived, understood, lived, grew. The very brevity of the statements was, I think, part of their strength. Whole volumes of truth and knowledge were compressed within them.

Indeed whole volumes, many of them, have been written expatiating on shards and splinters, aspects and fragments, implied within these themes, and others of similar nature. They tend to have exclamatory titles like 'Live In The Now!' or 'Understanding Life's Hidden Grammar!', and hundreds of them sit in publishers' lists or on bookshop shelves in the 'self-help' or 'psychology' sections, with cover banners that shriek 'This book can change your life!'

Unfortunately, it isn't true. An idea becomes adulterated when wilfully stretched to fit conventional book length, and couched in a style which lets its contents slide easily into the mind. The original substance is vitiated, because the material has been homogenised, pounded, and moulded into an easily swallowed analgesic or tranquilliser. Were it otherwise, the books would not sell. There is true gold to be mined in ideas such as 'Live in the Now!' – but only if we actually go down the mine ourselves. And of the millions who read self-help books, I'd guess it is only a rare few who do.

Only laziness, I think, plus the fact that popular writing accounts for part of my own livelihood, can explain why it has taken me so long to realise that most books of 'pop psychology' are designed, whether consciously or not, to help us avoid real thought. They give the impression that with the author's help we can 'know' something which will help solve life's difficulties, but too often the reader discovers that the book's contents cannot have purveyed quite the right knowledge, because after a while life is again as it was before. These 'change-your-life' books are drugs, really: first the hope, then the brief high, thereafter the hunt for the next hit.

I had a client like that once: an extreme case. She must have had dozens of self-help books on her shelves. Whatever I told her she said "Oh I know that" or "Yeah I read that", implying that if I couldn't give her any more than she already 'knew', she was wasting her time. What she needed, of course, was not the words but the inner experience. Guided imagery, which might have given that to her, was not an option because she'd "had that" too, and wanted something 'new'.

But why not stick with effective materials which are only as long as they need be, like (for instance) those two original statements? They've lasted over the centuries, and the power in them, when accessed, can fuel a journey beyond all expectation.

One reason, I'm sure, is that our society equates what is brief with what is insubstantial. Size matters. Length signals importance. And in spite of our ever-expanding digital media, we are still a book culture: indeed the length of books, probably *because* of computers, seems to be increasing. Another reason is that publishing is mostly determined by fashion – which means that of the many self-help books based on enduring knowledge, like the statements I've quoted, few are likely to last out a decade.

And in any case, how many books of psychological interest do we really need? If, as I'm arguing, most self-help books are usually no more than verbal aspirins, then perhaps real self-work would render most pop psychology titles unnecessary. We could do without them, together with the majority of text books describing new psychological techniques and 'schools'. For as readers of this journal know and the history of psychotherapy shows, once a new idea or technique has been formulated (and grasped) little else is necessary.

The subsequent flow of books on the subject has more to do with academic gamesmanship or furthering the writers' careers than anything else.

So what in my library would I save from a fire? Traditional materials (which in themselves are often primers for living, and thus at one level 'psychological'). Then myth and epic, folklore and story. I would need those, but could chuck out the many exegeses on them which clutter up my shelves at the moment. A good dictionary and encyclopaedia. Shakespeare. Goethe. Some poetry, Robert Burns topping the list. Some, but fewer, novels. Books, in fact, which have endured over time and transcend the categories. Modern writers, like Ted Hughes, whose work I think has the same survival potential.

And yet. I must now admit that useful and interesting ideas have been generated in my mind from all sorts of books, even trivial or bad books, and admit also that I enjoy the escapist, and sometimes illuminating, pleasures of novel-reading. So in a less high-minded mood – and in the absence of a fire – I find it hard to throw away almost any book.

And part of that difficulty, I think, is bound up with the reason why we have such great respect for books and their authors in the first place – any book, any author. So much so, that once we hear that 'so-and-so has written a book', even without knowing what that book is, most non-writers look at so-and-so again with renewed interest, even deference and respect. Could it be that our regard for books and writers is buried so deeply within us as to be an almost biological implant, from the days when knowledge was in the hands of the priests, and writing itself a sacred mystery?

18

The fountain of youth?
Just step out of time...

IN 2010 a group of elderly celebrities in reasonably good health went on a week's holiday – back to the mid-1970s. It was a time when the Bay City Rollers were hot, Margaret Thatcher was the first woman leader of the Parliamentary opposition, and the first cricket world cup was played at Lords. The group lived in a suburban house meticulously furnished and equipped in the style of the time – an era they all remembered as important for their lives and careers. They watched the TV programmes of the day, listened to the hit songs, ate the popular dishes of the period, slept in bedrooms which were as similar as their own bedrooms in 1975 as diligent researchers could make them, and had no mirrors to remind them of the present.

They all thoroughly enjoyed themselves, and emerged apparently rejuvenated. Newspaper editor Derek Jameson, for instance, who at the start couldn't even put his socks on unaided, hosted the final evening's dinner party, moving around with purpose and vigour. Eighty-eight-year-old Liz Smith was walking without sticks for the first time since three strokes 18 months earlier. And international cricket umpire Dickie Bird, deeply depressed after several very serious illnesses, found when tested that his memory had noticeably improved. He felt, he said, "like a different man". Even if only a temporary respite, everyone seemed taller and looked younger.

The 'holiday' was part of a BBC TV series called *The Young Ones*, based on a research study by Ellen Langer 30 years earlier. Langer, now a long-standing professor of psychology at Harvard, closeted her subjects in a monastery for five days in a recreated 1959, and before the study began, and again at the end of it, they underwent clinical tests. One would have expected the companionship and attention to have lifted their mood in any case – but there was far more to it. On several measures, they outperformed a control group that was encouraged, while remaining in the present day, to reminisce about life 20 years earlier. The experimental group were suppler, showed greater manual dexterity and stood taller. Their hearing, grip strength and manual dexterity had improved. Perhaps most improbable, so had their sight. Independent judges said they looked younger. The experimental subjects, Langer said, had "put their minds in an earlier time," and their bodies followed.

When Langer devised her study, the Western biomedical model was, for the most part, that mind and body ran on independent tracks. Her intention, pioneering at the time, was to show that the two were connected, and affected each other. Today we know more about how greatly the mind influences the body and are aware of the power of the placebo effect – which of course, doesn't only manifest via pills or clinical interventions. Indeed Langer predicted that the rekindling of her subjects' egos would be central to the reclamation of their bodies.

In fact anything that 'pleases' enlivens the mind. Even in old age we can, to a degree, regulate and invigorate our own psychological states. Through Robert Ornstein's 'multimind' model, for example, we can often banish a maladaptive state of mind and switch to another, more appropriate and positive, thus choosing whether our days are cloudy or sunny.

But pain, illness and hopelessness will nevertheless age us. Many of us know from experience that when we suffer a physical ailment, a psychological setback, or even extreme fatigue, we drag ourselves around, we feel heavy, we feel old, and a look in the mirror confirms it. And yet ... The mind really *is* stronger than the body. I remember reading about an injured World War II RAF fighter pilot with terrible third-degree burns over most of his body. The agony was unbearable. His only escape was to mentally divide his body in half, push all the pain into one half each morning and live in the other. The next day he would reverse the process. I tried it myself when severely ill and in great pain, and it certainly worked.

In the end, though, the body will age and die: it is of the earth, dense matter, susceptible to the ravages of time and disease. Eventually it will become too weak to hold us any longer. But the mind ... ah, the mind, that's a different matter! Minds are not bound by time. Minds soar, they dream, they learn, they travel through worlds, they choose their direction.

Most Human Givens therapists will have noticed, I'm sure, that even after a brief time in guided imagery, clients tend to emerge looking younger. And I wonder whether this is due, not only to the deep relaxation, but with time virtually disappearing, as it always seems to do when we work creatively, or meditate (if we do), or are transported by love, of something or someone – whenever we travel deep within our imaginations in fact. Could it be that ageing is slowed, even halted, at such moments?

Albert Einstein concluded in his later years that past, present and future exist simultaneously. But in that case, given that the underlying laws of physics work the same going forward as backwards, why does our experience of time run in only one direction? Why is it so much harder, mentally, before I sleep, to reverse direction and wind backwards through the events of the day than it is to project forwards towards the possible events of tomorrow?

In 2009 Sandu Popescu, professor of physics at the University of Bristol, together with a group of colleagues, suggested (in the journal *Physical Review*), that what stops the bi-directional flow of time is the way elementary particles intertwine when they interact: that is to say, they become quantum-mechanically entangled with their surroundings. Later research studies have confirmed this. In lay language, I suppose, you could say that in this way objects become 'earthed'.

I may not altogether understand the science, but I do know a good metaphor when I see one. Could it be, then, that an analogous entanglement is keeping our *minds* earthbound? Could, for instance, the Ten Commandments of the Bible, or the catalogue of the Seven Deadly Sins, be not so much finger wagging as technical instructions? If we managed, sufficiently, to avoid tangling our minds up in greed, lust, anger, laziness and so on, is it conceivable – as we read so often in the traditional literature – that this could be an element in springing the consciousness from time's prison? Now *there's* a prospect more enduring than, and light years away from, the painstaking recreation of the past.

19

A question of
identity

MY FRIEND Bernice, when we were 15, complained about her shyness and awkwardness at parties. "Mum says – 'just be yourself. But who am I?'" she wailed. "I don't *know* who I am. I am nobody!"

In all the years since, I have never forgotten her anguish and bafflement as she struggled to make sense of the fact that she didn't even know how to find out what her mother took for granted was the case: that Bernice knew how to be herself. Nor have I forgotten how scared she was, because if other people seemed sufficiently satisfied by what they saw as her, which she sensed was not really 'her' at all, then maybe she really *was* nobody, just an actor on stage, a character in a book. Not for nothing did Shakespeare put the words "to thine own self be true" in the mouth of a sanctimonious and foolish old man.

Even in Wonderland, when the Caterpillar demands of Alice "WHO ARE YOU?", she replies rather as Bernice would have done: "I–I hardly know, sir, just at present – at least I know who I WAS when I got up this morning, but I think I must have been changed several times since then." And when asked to explain herself: "I can't explain MYSELF, I'm afraid, sir, because I'm not myself, you see."

Bernice had learned well, from childhood on, the lessons of her teachers, her authority figures, her conditioning, and her society. She was clever, pretty, sociable, and appeared comfortable enough with herself in what you might call the ready-made clothes of our culture. Yet something else was also calling her, even if at this stage not yet loudly or insistently enough for her to be more than vaguely troubled by it.

Over the years I've heard many others worrying over that same dissonance of both being there yet at the same time not really being there at all: indeed at certain points in my life I have been one of them. And from both clients and friends I have heard individuals report that they felt "annihilated" or "powerless" or "fighting furious" when, under certain circumstances, they were ignored by partner, friend or boss, or put down in a particularly demeaning way – as if, in fact, they were nobody.

Increasingly, psychotherapists are realising that emotions aroused by an originating event in childhood will encode as a pattern which, when triggered later on by a matching pattern, causes the automatic arousal of identical feelings. But what interests me is that often what seems to lie underneath all these feelings is sheer fear – engendered by the realisation that suddenly I am revealed as what I really am. Nothing. Nobody. No matter how many disabling emotions we chase down the corridors of our being, whatever guise they come in and whatever we call them, for many people that fear of nothingness seems to lie under them all. The existentialists, who had a few good ideas, called those totally emptied episodes "existential angst".

At such defining moments the exemplars and heroes of myth, epic, story and religious mysteries alike sometimes find themselves in front of the high gate which opens onto the next stage in their journey, and are challenged there to state their essential identity. In fact from Mozart's *Magic Flute* to our own still small voice at midnight, the moment arrives when wayfarers (and we are all such) are asked, as Tom Bombadil asks in *The Lord of the Rings*, "and who are you – alone, yourself, and nameless?"

One can often see the fear of that nameless emptiness driving people forward to high achievement, as they determinedly deflect their own and others' attention away from the abyss of non-entity they feel beneath them. The same drive also seems to me to lie under many distorting psychological states, such as the us-and-them phenomenon, where people bolster their identities, endowing themselves with feelings of specialness and belonging by excluding, or in extreme cases eliminating, 'inferior' or 'alien' others.

I hear that my friend Bernice went on to great success in life, and have often wondered whether she confronted those fears of being nobody; indeed whether she saw that fear, and the other strong emotions in which we can become lost, as the phantoms they are. And I wonder, too, given her personality, whether she would have defused them simply by accepting, relaxing into, and passing through the gate.

Indeed we read in Homer's *Odyssey* that after many adventures Odysseus, having lost all his ships and crew, loses the last remnant of all, the plank of wood to which he has been clinging, in the watery tumult between the whirlpool Scylla and the abyss Charybdis. Now truly 'nobody but himself', with nothing left at all, he is washed up naked on the final island he will visit, and there tells his story to the king of that place. Then he is given new clothes, a new boat, and a new crew to sail him – while he sleeps – back to his home at last.

I think that many people believe they are embarking on an analogous odyssey when they enter psychoanalysis or one of the psychotherapies. They are seeking to discover the answer to those deepest of human questions, 'who am I?', 'where do I come from, and what am I for?', thinking that by stripping themselves psychologically naked and telling their therapist their own story, they too will emerge with new clothes, a new boat and crew – and be sailed, like Ulysses, to their home destination.

But I also think it is a mistake to attribute the functions of either the search or the finding to psychotherapy. The problems of Prince Tamino, hero of the *Magic Flute*, for instance, are resolved in the first five minutes of the story, and *then* his journey begins. In my understanding, while therapy may stabilise the ground, clear the path, even make the quest more feasible, it is not nor cannot be the means by which the journey is made, nor the destination found.

However I see this confusion again and again: both in clients who hope they will emerge from therapy with their true identity discovered and their lives somehow solved, and in therapists who believe they are 'soul-makers', as one recently expressed it to me. A girl I encountered in the 60s unwittingly satirised the shallowness of these shoppers and sellers alike: "I did a death and transfiguration workshop last week", she told me, with great sincerity, "and I liked it so much I think I'll teach it!"

20

...You don't know
what you've got...

IF WORLD WAR II were to happen now, how would we cope? In a society in which many believe that instant gratification and the acquisition of material goods are essential for living, would qualities of optimism, patience, making do, endurance and sacrifice have to be re-learned?

For many, I feel sure, the lessons would be harsh and painful. Yet within living memory the concepts I've mentioned were 'givens' of British society, put there by previous generations in earlier, more stable days, like money in the bank. And by now, much of it spent.

Growing up in the police state which was apartheid South Africa, I thanked my lucky stars when in my very early 20s I arrived in Britain, a haven of tolerance, fair play and social cohesiveness. But very soon after that I was watching with dismay how people lacking my South African experience didn't prize, or even *see*, what they had, and took for granted principles of justice, privacy, and individual freedom to which generations had devoted themselves and often died for.

For example, during my early years in Britain, bureaucracy was thought of as a European disease. We congratulated ourselves that all the Kafkaesque bureaucratic insanities we saw or read about could never happen on these islands. Then we somehow lost the basic understanding that circumstances alter cases – and the flexibility which had protected us disappeared.

Another example. Viennese doctors in the 19th century would simply wipe their gory hands on already bloody coats as they went from practising or demonstrating on cadavers to examining women about to give birth.

Unsurprisingly, mortality was sky high. Then obstetrician Ignatz Semmelweiss discovered that his patients would usually survive if he simply washed his hands between examining each of them.

In attempting to get his colleagues to do the same, this pioneer of medical prophylaxis waged a lonely and punishing one-man crusade. It drove him insane in the end, but today we see him as the father of preventive medicine. Because of his insights and persistence, millions of lives have been saved all over the world. Yet today we seem to have forgotten all this, and are struggling to maintain elementary hygiene in many of our hospitals.

We also seem to have forgotten how we got to the moon. I've read that following the Apollo 17 mission in 1972, a set of blueprints for the Saturn booster, the only rocket with enough thrust to send a manned lunar payload on its way, was somehow *thrown away*. The project directors were moving offices at the time, and in any case attention had turned to designing a rocket to put man on Mars – which all these years later, has thus far not happened.

So much regrettable loss, both great and small. I remember a time when we 'handled' snow on the road simply by putting chains on our tyres. A time when cookers were so simple that they lasted for decades. A time when many people fixed their own cars because the engineering was fairly straightforward. Now, however, the electronics are so complicated that the moment anything goes wrong, car-owners must call in the professionals.

In William J. Miller's science-fiction novel *A Canticle for Leibowitz*, which takes place centuries after a disastrous devastation of our planet, the little knowledge which has been salvaged is in the hands of the church. At one point a bumbling young monk stumbles across a printed circuit in a fall-out shelter – and devotes his life to making flowery illuminated copies of this "holy relic".

In my opinion, that could so easily happen even today. In spite of all our talk, society's brilliant technological advances are not our individual property. We could lose them in a disaster. But the real disaster would be to forget the core principles underlying them. Were that to happen, then as with William Miller's young monk, magical thinking could once again take over from knowledge.

Even though centuries ago King Canute wonderfully demonstrated that it was impossible to command the waves, the realities of daily life can still drown in a sea of wishful thinking. Though we are aware in our saner moments that children generally fare better in stable families, and that women and men, though certainly equal are definitely not the same, we often hear this knowledge categorically denied.

Psychotherapists, along with many others, know that 'perfectionist' individuals inevitably come a cropper. But so do 'perfectionist' societies such as ours. We are fed on a diet of direct and indirect 'commercials' telling us that the 'ideal' is achievable, and that it's out there waiting for all of us.

In such a context, it can often be hard, especially when young, to discriminate between the optimum potential in a situation and the 'ideal'. Consequently, in many departments of life, battalions of crazed experimentalists in search of perfection rush in to change things, over and over again, demolishing precious knowledge as they go.

But there is always a distance between the optimum and the perfect in this world – a concept lost to our society, perhaps, when religion as a lingua franca was lost. I am not formally religious myself, but think that we have forfeited a cornucopia of powerful concepts embedded in the religious traditions, and are the poorer for it. Among these are gratitude for whatever we have, considering our neighbours' needs as well as our own, a striving towards improvement – and an effort to see beyond the surfaces.

It's the constant cry of the old: "It's all getting worse!" But, old myself now, I see past the grumpiness and fogeyism into the kernel of the cry: the longing for present and future generations to take care – not of the hand-washing but of the reason for it; not of opposition to bureaucracy for its own sake but in order to preserve flexibility; not of outward appearances, but to protect what is essential within. The outward form will – must – change many times over, but the essence needs to be guarded. However most young people can't see into the heart of things fast enough, because they are still in the process of accumulating the experiences that will teach them that.

Perhaps we could study some of the ways simpler societies maintain and recycle essential knowledge. In many of these the old are expected to spend a lot of time with the young, transmitting the community's treasured knowledge, the patterns of which are held in metaphors and stories. Elders arrange appropriate initiatory experiences, which will change forever the understanding of those who go through them. And in whatever they do, they have no need to be popular, only effective.

Could we cultivate that sort of 'ecological' attitude to knowledge in our more complex society? If not, then a lyric of Joni Mitchell's will remain only too true: "... you don't know what you've got till it's gone."

21

When words can't say it

MY OLD FRIEND from childhood, Paula, has argued with me for decades. She insists, as many intellectuals do, that if you can't say something in precise words, then whatever it is does not exist.

Paula has a verbal brilliance and agility I have never seen equalled. She loathes religion, and fervently worships at the altar of Western science. She also seems compelled to steer me into positions where I'll say that certain realities are beyond words. Then she demolishes me in the argument, because in the face of her scorn and fire power all my words disappear.

Yet in spite of Paula and like-minded reductionists, experience tells me that although unsayable perceptions, experiences and entities may be signposted or evoked by words, and although we can ride towards them by way of metaphor, certain states, and certain ideas, have an independent existence.

I think 'intention' is like this. The long-winded attempts by philosophers over centuries, and psychologists in more recent times, to define intention, illustrate how impossible it is to pin this concept down. In my own experience, it is actually more like a physical sensation, so substantial and real that when focussed and concentrated in the mind, will pour into whatever situation it is directed at.

For instance, I was recently asked to see Blanche, the five-year-old daughter of a former client. Her father had died ten months before. Since then she had become very clingy, was having frequent bowel 'accidents', and at school so lacked attention that she had been transferred to a less able group.

Because I have no clinical experience of children this young, I recommended an excellent therapist who did. But Blanche's mother had done well in therapy with me, and was determined she wouldn't take the child to anyone else. Reluctantly, though uttering cautions, I agreed to have a go.

Before the session, I spent a few moments – again as I am sure all therapists do in extremis, and some as a matter of course – focusing my intention to be helpful, aiming it to be as 'clean', and to soar as 'high', as I could manage. When I do that I can almost taste the intention, it coheres into what feels real, impersonal and objective, and during the session 'it', whatever it is, seems to ride out on the back of whatever words I might say. I'm still working, consciously, as carefully and skilfully as I can, but the concentrated intention is also somehow operating like radar, determining the shape the work takes in the session, influencing what comes into my mind, affecting the flow between me and the client.

But even so the session with Blanche was a shambles. Most of the time she clung tightly to her mother. I was virtually invisible. From time to time she leapt off her mother's lap and raced round the room, hectically picking up objects and slamming them down. I tried a story but couldn't catch her attention. I offered toys, but her interest was fleeting. Several times I threw a little rubber ball at her, which she didn't catch. So now and then, in desperation, I spoke out, into the air, all the various metaphors and images I thought could be liberating.

I told myself that maybe we'd connect next time – if there was one. But her mother didn't call until two months later, when she rang for a 'top-up' appointment for herself. Nervously, I asked how Blanche was. "Oh she's fine, great", she said nonchalantly. "Messing in her pants?" "Not since she saw you." "And her attention span?" "OK now. She's back in her old class at school." "Really?" "Yes, the teacher says she's doing very well."

I imagine many therapists have had an experience like this, so staggering that we never forget it. Truly, I had done *nothing*. I was irrelevant and incompetent throughout the session. So I have decided that two invisible factors must have been at work. First, the intention to help so powerfully concentrated inside me, and second, the mother's equally powerful certainty that I would be able to do so.

All writers who are serious, not hacks, know from experience that when they put a lot of thought into what they are trying to communicate, and then boil it down and boil it down until sometimes few of the original sentences remain, none of that thought is lost. It is like pouring the essence of poetry into prose. My husband calls this homeopathic writing – the tiniest tincture reduced from the original, concentrated and expressed with the greatest possible care and accuracy, somehow communicates it all.

But then I realise that even when *not* so accurately condensed or reflected, something of the original still communicates. For instance when I was young I read Fitzgerald's *Omar Khayyam*, and took from it, I discovered years later with wider reading and a far more accurate translation, a meaning vastly different from what Fitzgerald had set on the page, and more in tune with Omar Khayyam's original meaning and intention.

So perhaps something of the essence of a strongly concentrated idea can, as it were, be decanted to a greater or lesser extent into any container which is open and waiting – whether through the utterances of great poets, visionaries, and storytellers, or Fitzgerald's inexact rendering, or my clumsy mouthing of metaphors. The wordless reality to be communicated is like light from a far star. But what illuminates the dark in our local streets, be it lamp, torch, candle or match, shares the nature of that other light. Perhaps, also, little Blanche was a natural, open recipient.

Paula is right in this respect – if words can be used at all, they should be used with precision. But I think realities beyond and behind words determine the power and quality of all creative work, therapy included. The better the therapy-model, the better results the therapeutic cohort will achieve as a whole, but therapy is always more than just a method to be applied, and all the research shows that the quality of the individual therapist is the most important factor in any therapy.

Indeed it seems to me that there are times when all a therapist can do is detach from method and stay calm in the face of ambiguity and confusion, allowing wordless factors, focussed intention among them, to play their part. For it is often when we feel quite helpless, and abandon any illusion of 'control', that our most creative and effective work is done.

22

The norm is
not the rule

RECENTLY I watched a five-year-old girl playing snakes and ladders, unselfconsciously altering the rules to suit herself, and being allowed to win by her gently understanding 22-year-old opponent.

Watching them reminded me that children under six, while striving their utmost to understand the world, still seem to be making up many of their own rules – but by eight they have learned to follow, indeed want to follow, whatever the rules may be or say. Then as the children mature they learn discrimination, and are increasingly able to select when to obey rules and when they need breaking. So I think our society must largely be peopled by adult five-year-olds, because we too make up most of the rules to suit ourselves.

On the same day as the snakes and ladders game I saw a celebrity actress quoted in a magazine: "I strive to be flawless in my work and my life". And I met a new client who said: "All I want is people to behave properly to me, instead of messing me up".

But you and I know that can't be. As the Muslims say, "only God is perfect" – which means that the job is already taken, thank goodness, and therefore we are not required to do any more than our absolute best. But the actress who strives to be flawless is, like every perfectionist, simply inventing her own rules and setting herself up for failure. So too is a former client of mine, a well-known actress, sane in all other respects, I think, but who was absolutely convinced, until I disabused her, that she could not only control everything in her own life, including the behaviour of others, but also, even, the weather.

I wish I could remember who wrote "we should listen carefully to nature, not tell nature how to behave" – because not listening, I believe, is what is keeping us infantilised. Of course there are many ways of looking at any truth, but what I see right now, somewhat to my surprise, is that under the greed which wrenches 'how it is' into 'how we want it' there lies nothing less than a lack of love – and of gratitude, love's companion.

The evidence is everywhere. Very recently farmers flew in the face of nature, and on an industrial scale fed their animals the ground-up remains of even their diseased fellows. But by turning herbivorous cattle into cannibals, they were violating the implicit contract, understood so well in simpler societies, of gratitude and good husbandry by humans towards the animals who will ultimately die for them. And this happened in spite of the fact that we had known for decades (in another department of discourse) that certain degenerative and brain diseases in humans are caused solely by cannibalism.

Recently, too, we have watched the rules of common sense be rewritten, by people coldly selling houses to those they knew couldn't afford them; and by others equally coldly selling the consequent debts on – and on and on – in a lucrative game of pass the parcel. There was certainly no love or care for those at the bottom of this house of cards – just as many older, influential and experienced people in our society clearly have no love for the young and untested. Instead of guiding their growth and development, they rewrite the natural order and start imitating the young themselves.

Again, though much in the feminist revolution was and remains useful and necessary, some innate differences between male and female natures, well understood by our great-grandmothers and generations of women before them, became by decree, so to speak, no longer to be tolerated. Neuroscience has since confirmed much of the traditional understanding, but in the teeth of the evidence some of us still impose 'rules' more to our liking. To a certain extent biology can be overridden, but if we implacably extract from our loved ones the behaviour we expect or would prefer, then perhaps we are simply turning them into trained animals – and who wants to live with a creature like that?

TV executives and producers, too, show no love for their viewers when they defend the gratuitous nastiness and violence they put on our screens, saying – in the teeth of all the research – that there is no evidence that viewers are affected. But hard-nosed advertisers will pay far more than the cost of an hour's documentary for just ninety seconds on the small screen, because they *know* it will influence people to buy their wares. Most of them, too, have no love for the consumers they manipulate in order to get their money.

And only blindness to the rule that 'whatever we do affects others' can enable a pretty girl to sway down the street in fashionably tight, flesh-exposing clothes, so insulated within her own narcissism (fed by the aforementioned advertising industry) that she is shocked and offended if some disadvantaged or greedy individual makes a grab for what he sees as 'the goods'. She certainly does not realise that she is valuable and so must take care of herself – or see that by taking care she helps these others too.

Even the law of 'God', whatever that word represents to any individual, is commonly rewritten to say – answer my prayers and stop bad things happening if you want to earn my love. There may be valid reasons to reject religion, but delivering a one-sided contract to 'God' was never among them.

For rather a long time we five-year-olds have been bending the world to our individual whims, regarding our wants as entitlements. But in the end, the hectic drive for success, prestige, money, power or instant pleasure, bring dwindling satisfactions. And so wherever we look we see the disintegration of love in our society, at the same time as we howl for it in our songs and popular culture. But high expectations encourage not only a culture of debt and cynicism. They increase the emptiness within the heart.

Perhaps we have been so comfortable, so protected from the basic winds of nature, for so long, that we thought we could get away with violating natural 'rules' forever. In this, we ignored another rule: whatever the time lag between behaviour and consequences, at some point there will be a reckoning. Nature always restores the ecological balance, and green shoots grow right next to the dead wood she has destroyed. I've heard many people saying: "I always knew it was just a matter of time before the bubble burst", and "How on earth did we think we could get away with it?" Coming down to earth, they say, is a good and necessary thing. Unthinkable catastrophes, they say, are close at hand.

In this they see a hopeful, if difficult, future. They believe that in a culture of "less", people will count for more; that rather than being acted upon by faceless statutory bodies, the current development of 'transitional communities' is already sparking 'human' co-operation between ordinary individuals. I'm not holding my breath, but if they are right, then the actress with her illusion of flawlessness and the client wanting to bend others to her will, could find their lives radically altered – tougher perhaps, but more real and more fulfilling.

23

Science yes – but
metaphor too

WESTERN SCIENTISTS are currently hunting for a 'theory of everything'. If they find one, I suppose it will supply for our society the kind of meaning which in the distant past was provided by myth. That too was an explanation of everything, a metaphorical tale encompassing both the natural world and the cosmos.

I think of myths as stories which clothe huge, comprehensive metaphors, extruded from another dimension into ours, so that their visible aspects in this dimension can sometimes be joined in unexpected ways. Only certain parts of the tale can fit within familiar perceptions. The rest takes place off-stage, rather like one of those pencil-and-paper puzzles which can only be solved by going right outside the given frame.

This straddling of dimensions inevitably makes myths strange and confusing, with loose ends and unclear events all over the place. By contrast, I think a 'theory of everything' would have a heroic, systematic tidiness. And would such a theory hold for as long as myths have held? Einstein's "certainties", for instance, raised problems from the start. And Stephen Hawking, for instance, routinely reconsiders aspects of his theory.

However, I am told some biologists have proposed Richard Dawkins's idea of the "meme" as a mental 'theory of everything'. Dawkins postulates the 'meme' as a unit of cultural transmission or imitation – anything from shifts in the pronunciation of certain words, to tunes and catch-phrases, fashions and ideas, beliefs and religions. He contends that when we imitate someone else – and we are mimetic creatures – something is passed on, again and again, and takes on a life of its own. It competes to get into human brains, and then jumps from brain to brain, propagating itself round the culture or round the world. The implication is that we hardly exist, if at all; there is no self – just memes using us as vehicles for their own survival.

The idea of the 'meme' is, I think, a description of the part as the whole. But the major discoveries of science can seem more universally applicable than that – more like special physical instances of a greater metaphor. Though we may not understand the maths, the pattern still impinges on us.

Even physics, one of the 'hardest' of the sciences, yields resonant metaphors. Indeed Coleridge, so I've read, would often go to scientific lectures in his search for metaphors. And author Philip Pullman does the same. It's fertile ground. For instance, physics is in essence the study of various forms of energy, and we often refer to our own feelings in terms of electricity or hydraulics. So we say we feel low, high, pressured, drained, charged or brimming with energy.

Metaphors of relativity are also found wherever we look, from Einstein's own joke definition of "relativity: when you're waiting to see your girlfriend times goes slowly, when you're with her time goes fast": to the fact that our own difficulties seem lighter once we recognise the heavy loads others have to bear.

Osmosis too provides metaphors of absorption and permeability, and suggests a particularly effective means of communicating know-how and information. Indeed, this is the basis of apprenticeship. I also know a professional training school which regularly includes a small number of disadvantaged, or members of the 'awkward squad', in its intake. Experience has taught them that such people, while too few to destabilise the group, can be absorbed, affected and changed by the general positive atmosphere of learning and co-operation.

Then there's Le Chatelier's principle. It states that if some stress is brought to bear upon a system in equilibrium, a change occurs, such that the equilibrium is displaced in a direction which tends to undo the effect of the stress. Just so. We call it the survival instinct.

Newton's Laws of Motion are rich with metaphor. For example: if a body is at rest it will remain at rest. Well, sleep begets sleep, as the old wives' saying has it, referring to babies, and laziness too. As the saying goes, "the appetite grows on what it feeds".

Newton also says that if a body is in motion it will remain in motion in a straight line unless acted upon by an externally impressed force. Again, we often enact that law in our own lives. As in the old maxim, as in literature, as in the film *Groundhog Day*, he who does not learn from his mistakes is bound to repeat them – until there's an almighty collision with the facts of life, a crash which forces us to change direction.

Heisenberg's uncertainty principle – increasing detail on one parameter will inevitability lead to loss of acuity on another – helps us realise how what we see is changed by the very act of looking at it, an understanding crucial in psychology, as in most domains of life. And Boyle's Law (gas expands to fill the space available) has generated its light-hearted but no less accurate equivalent in Parkinson's Law – work expands to fill the time available for its completion. In fact C. Northcote Parkinson actually based his satiric dictum on Boyle's Law and published it as a humorous essay in *The Economist* in 1955. In the therapy room, too, I can watch emotional states expand to fill the mental space available for them.

Metaphors from scientific principles, then, are easy to find. But are they no more than memes, as Dawkins contends? Indeed does he think there is any difference between a metaphor and a meme? For if our mental furniture were comprised of nothing but 'memes', then at a stroke the idea of the existence of multi-faceted metaphors and their huge webs of meaning would be destroyed.

Though Dawkins doesn't himself propose his idea as quite the theory of everything, he has said he would be pleased to see it become a "proper hypothesis of the human mind". However an ancient, well-known story deals a gentle but devastating blow to this, or any other, contender for a comprehensive theory. In the tale, different people each examine different parts of an elephant and describe it in terms of their own knowledge and preoccupations – feeling the trunk, one concludes it's a hose-pipe; feeling an ear, another concludes it's a fan; another who feels the leg, likens it to a pillar; yet another, with a hand on the back, is convinced it's some sort of throne. None see the whole elephant.

Of course a metaphor or tale which is not actively or consciously experienced within the mind, *can* be passed on as a meme, in an associative, mimetic way. And herd animals that we are, this is what seems to be going on much of the time – memes circulating within the various partial views of the elephant. But there are also times when a metaphor is vividly experienced within the imagination, and a wordless essence of meaning comes alive. At such times, which I'm sure we've all experienced, the perception of the metaphor is in no way passively mimetic but active, creative, individual – and a lantern on reality.

24

Getting stuck and digging out

CERTAIN SOCIETIES, I read, use the same word for both slaves and domesticated animals, and in many ways I think this idea applies in ours. But it is we who are the domesticated creatures – slaves to systems, social and political agencies, jobs, mortgages, routines. Most of us settle into these straitjackets so comfortably, on the whole, that even a minor disruption is disproportionately destabilising, an unwelcome reminder of the constraints which bind us.

In fact the urge to settle things seems built-in. Settle the mortgage, see the children settled, settle into the job, settle who will be prime minister. We've settled down at last, we say thankfully, after a period of turmoil. We may like to be blown by the wind when young, light and flexible, but later most of us are more comfortable when events, and even friends, are predictable. The computer works. The car starts. We go out Saturday nights. The regular salary arrives. We are on top of things.

'Settled', in fact, brings with it the illusion of certainty and self-sufficiency. However that is an illusion, and one which can disconnect us not only from other people, but also from the origins and sources of the events we must deal with. And then, isolated and lacking information, it is too easy to be obstructive without realising the damage we do.

For instance a close relative of mine, Simon, is 80 and has been ill for some years. He is looked after by his mother-in-law, Edith, who is 85. She is lively, conscientious and caring. But when Simon's wife, who works all day, recently enquired from social services whether she could get some financial help for her mother, the request was refused – because Edith is "too old to be a carer".

It's as if we are all marooned on tiny islands in a lake of amnesia and ignorance – most of the time believing that the island we live on is all there is. We forget – or have no experience of – the connections between things: how one step leads to another, and then to another. As far as that bureaucrat, well settled in his or her job, is concerned, he is enslaved by marks on a piece of paper saying that Edith can't be a carer because she is too old. So as far as he is concerned she isn't, end of story – even though across the lake of ignorance, where *she* lives, she really *is* one, and must continue to be, with or without the Council's help.

We live so far from the ground, in fact, that most of us have little or no concept of how machines work – and think they do so, as Edward de Bono once pointed out many children thought, because we press a button. And few of us think of visualising, or finding out, how a table is made, say, or how the food placed on it is cooked.

In fact the settled state is like theatre – an illusion lasting for a limited period. We, the audience, don't know or care what went before or will come after. Settled in our seats, the play is delightful and convincing. We have not the foggiest idea about the panic at dress rehearsal, last-minute difficulties with costumes, the intricacies of production. In the nick of time, touch and go, it all came together to create the illusion which entertains us. Now *that's* what we paid up for when we bought our tickets.

But what if there's a fire in the theatre and the show suddenly stops? From one moment to the next, the illusion of solid ground beneath our feet goes up in smoke.

In his marvellous autobiography, *An Anthropology of Everyday Life* (published by Doubleday Books), that exceptional observer of the hidden dimensions of cultures, anthropologist Edward T. Hall, describes how as a young man in the early 1930s he lived and worked on what in those days he was allowed to call an Indian 'reservation'. The area was not yet adapted to cars, and "getting the car stuck and digging it out" were as much part of day-to-day living there "as getting up and having breakfast".

"Newcomers would get angry and frustrated", he writes, "at finding themselves stuck in the mud, mired in a sand dune or hung up on a high centre. There would be a great gnashing of teeth, swearing, surveying the situation, slamming of car doors, spinning the wheels – all of which only made things worse. Somehow, if you knew how to drive, things like this were not supposed to happen. Then they would curse the reservation. What sort of a country was this with no roads anyway? The status of the male ego was at stake…"

Anthropologists often describe such wild and excessive behaviour in members of the 'primitive' cultures they study. But when even small things go wrong in our own neck of the woods, I have watched myself and other settled members of our 'superior' society conducting ourselves in just that way.

Everyone got stuck, says Hall, day after day, over and over again in a single journey. Sometimes he would have to walk 15 miles or more to a destination if time was needed for the mud, mired up to the hubcaps, to dry out round his car. He learned that if there was a dirty, difficult, complex, crucial job to do, "one should forgo the temptation of a quick fix, roll up one's sleeves (figuratively or literally), take a deep breath, and do what is needed … and do it properly." Once, for instance, he had to dig out muddy ruts for several hundred feet and fill them with sand from a nearby dune, (carried in his Stetson hat), so that the car's wheels could sit on the sand-packed ruts, and he wouldn't get stuck again twenty feet down the road. It took hours, as digging himself out in one way or another often did, but in the end he knew he was really free.

People in settled societies like ours are very interested in what people have, such as money, property, status, and stuff. But we are relatively unaware of what people are. Hall learned on the reservation "the things one must know, the skills one must have, and the character traits that are essential, in order to get around". He says it helped him to connect with the world as it really is, "not as it has been altered by human beings to make life easier."

We have all, often, been unsettled, realising suddenly and uneasily that we are slaves, not masters, of systems, circumstances, habits. We know from personal experience that life's theatre can be abruptly stopped, temporarily or permanently. But whenever we manage it, we like being 'sorted' rather than 'settled'; having our feet on the ground rather than planted firmly in the air. Getting stuck and digging out, as Hall himself points out, is a metaphor for life.

25

Going, going...
gone with the flow

CHANGE, as we know, is the only constant. Everything wears out – my shoes, his opinions, her diet plans, most 'incontrovertible' facts, every kingdom and empire, your patience. The sun and the stars may reliably shine for us – but from their point of view the story is the same. Things wax, things wane, and in the end their time is up.

Even the meaning of what we think and speak washes in and out of the containers fashioned to hold and reflect it. The very same words, phrases, or sentences can blaze with glory or collapse into sheer silliness.

Living in such endless upheaval, no wonder we sometimes seize up with tension and worry. And then someone airily says: "oh, stop worrying, just go with the flow", which may actually be good advice, but which is also meaningless and irritating – because a valid and valuable idea has been reduced to a mere slogan.

Go with the flow? Hang on a moment. What flow? Where? When? Always? Before breakfast or after? Assuming it's a good idea, am I even equipped to go with this flow? What if it hurls me down the rapids without a canoe? And *how* does one go with it? Well, certainly not just by hearing that phrase spoken as slogan, watchword or incantation.

When athletes enter 'the flow' (which these days they call 'the zone') they describe how they literally can't put a foot wrong. They make and break records; they seem to be simultaneously 'there' and 'not there', held in a tide of events in which ordinary thought itself is set aside. But athletes don't just go with the flow. They have carefully prepared their bodies and minds. And they also know that the state is not theirs to command or even predict.

For those of us who are not athletes the experience may occur when we let personal wishes and preoccupations go, and yield to the rhythm of events – but only, I think, after plans, preparations and sincere efforts have been made. Many, probably most, of us have experienced this state; it may even have proved a turning point in our lives. But it's not a common, everyday occurrence.

So the flip injunction, 'just go with the flow', is an empty shell. I have unpacked only a fragment of an outer edge of this subtle concept found in many of the traditions, including Taoism, in an attempt to show how rich complexities – and rich simplicities too, for that matter – such as the phrase under discussion, can be reduced to a Christmas cracker motto.

It is a terrible hazard, this degradation of meaning, and it is caused by using language carelessly, even callously, sloganising something which is really beyond words and which can only barely be brought into this form. I have even seen words written with masterful caution and foresight, carefully protected by their context and hedged around with subtle caveats, stolen by 'admirers' and sloganised into 'the truth'. The posters outside London theatres provide a crude analogy. A newspaper reviewer might have said "we had hoped for a brilliant show, but this wasn't it" and the poster shrieks "brilliant show". Sloganising takes words which in their original context have the potential to raise and transform, and uses them to do their very opposite: to reduce and condition. Words thus appropriated and then mouthed unconsciously can no longer fly to their target, but become crippled, earthbound, communicating the very opposite of their original intention.

Shakespeare brilliantly sent up the idea that words always mean the same, no matter the context or who says them. In a speech in *Hamlet*, he puts a whole cascade of nominally wise and powerful sayings – including "This above all, to thine own self be true ..." – into the mouth of a hypocritical old fool, and thereby lets us see how nonsensical, in some contexts, even resonant ideas can become.

Possibly the only proper place for the slogan or motto is in advertising. Slogans do their work perfectly when honest, witty, and memorable, as for example the current Tesco slogan for their internet order and delivery service: 'You shop, we drop'. That's what they undertake to do, and very useful too. No hidden messages. But more frequently advertising slogans operate a subtext of ideas we are not even aware of, but which can nevertheless coerce and destabilise us.

The implications behind the Clairol slogan 'because I'm worth it', for example, raise real anxieties in vulnerable individuals; calling into question their shaky sense of status and self-worth. Such slogans are the consumer society's ammunition: by keeping people insecure they are a soft touch for the next new product, and the next and the next. And if you think I am laying it on a bit thick, you should hear some of the worries expressed in my therapy room by bright, pretty young women who have been got at about their hair, their shape, even their essential 'value'.

Mechanical repetition does, of course, have its place. Once we know how to drive, we actually *need* our reactions to be automatic. Children learn their 'times table' to have this specific manipulation of numbers automatically on call. And Hassidic Jews, I'm told, put their clothes on, buttoning and zipping them in strict order – automatising the 'lower' action in the hopes of freeing the attention for something 'higher'.

But when something higher is automatised and thus brought down ... then we are all the losers. Stale metaphors no longer light our minds; stale phrases pass us by. To be kept fresh, ideas need to be reformulated. Otherwise even the word of God himself (so to speak) can end up as if written on a cardboard placard.

Some people require an idea to be 'original' before they will concede it value. But this simply indicates a jaded palate. Nothing worthwhile is ever original. It is simply formulated in a new way for a new generation, and needs to be if it is going to be registered. The enduring stories of the world are constant in their essence, but dressed up time and again in new clothing. As the proverb has it: the more things change the more they stay the same.

Perhaps this is one reason why it is useful to keep certain ideas and materials away from public gaze. Heard too soon, they have no meaning. And when they are ready to be heard, the words may miss their mark because they are just too familiar. Many such phrases circulate in our language as slogans, sayings, watchwords, mottos, call them what you will. 'Count your blessings' is one. 'Love makes the world go round' is another.

Mostly, their effect is vacuous or annoying. We have heard them thousands of times before. But if anyone finds the substance within such phrases for themselves, consciously, it can be as if those familiar words were being said for the very first time, and their meaning can tear a veil from the eyes.

26

The soft life
has its limits

A FRIEND WHO heads a prestigious American institute for cognitive therapy tells me that on the day following the World Trade Centre atrocity, on 9/11, they received over 4000 enquiries about therapy for post-traumatic stress disorder. The personnel at the Centre had to explain, over and over again, that this condition really *was* post-traumatic. Symptoms had to appear first – you couldn't wipe them out ahead of time. That same day, my friend said, she had called her daughter, who lives in a war zone and asked how she was. "Oh fine", said her daughter cheerfully. "I can hear bombing in the hills, but I'm just fine."

This conversation surfaced in my mind during a recent lecture by sociologist Dr Peter Marsh, whose contention was – as mine is here – that never in the history of our evolution have we lived in such a risk-free environment, and never have we been so risk averse.

It is far from an original thought that while western societies are fortunate enough to live well and safely, this welcome achievement has in certain ways made us soft. Extreme hardship and risk have been eliminated, freeing up our time and capacity. But we use up these gains by focussing, as if our lives depended on it, on more trivial worries instead! Living safely has caused us, for the most part, to live within a much narrower band of experience.

This is why many of us have little understanding of really hard lives. A black South African friend once told me that as a child she wondered why white people in trains sat quietly in well-appointed compartments with wide seats, while in the black carriages people jammed noisily together, sometimes two or three deep on top of each other. With the clear perception and ungrudging generosity of children, she decided that whites were fragile and had to be looked after; they couldn't cope with the conditions her people lived under.

An incident in Jason Elliot's wonderful *Afghanistan, An Unex-*

pected Light, also highlights this factor of limited experience. Without any warning, he and his mujuhedin companions find themselves under Soviet attack. The others dive for cover, but Elliot's instincts are unschooled and he wanders through the hail of fire as if in a dream. As bullets suddenly crack loudly in his ears, someone tackles him rugby-style and drags him into cover, saving his life. Pressed up hard against three men, shells flying overhead, he feels the person next to him trembling. 'They are even more terrified than me', he thinks. Then he looks at their faces – and realises they are convulsed with laughter.

Laughter is a wonderful release from whatever is imprisoning us, and I wonder if, just as hardship produces glorious, whole-hearted peals of belly-laughter, the jeering, vicious humour our society has developed in recent years is a symptom of the general comfort and absence of sadness in our lives. For I have seen many times how often people familiar with sadness and danger can be generous to others and hugely relish life's pleasures, finding them in more and simpler and cleaner places than many others of us do.

I briefly thought, along with many others, that there might somehow be a seismic shift in perspective after the 9/11 atrocity; that those attacks would concentrate our minds wonderfully; and that I for one would probably lose at least half my therapy clients overnight. But though we are aware that our world has become more risky, so far the mindset hasn't noticeably changed. And while the greater proportion of those who come to see me are grappling with the fallout from genuine damage and trauma, others seem depressed and anxious about nothing very real, though their misery and suffering are genuine enough.

It's as if we have replaced the dangers we have conquered with paper tigers; illusory dangers. At the lunatic end we even find victim support groups for addiction to, of all things, caffeine, a psychologist who has made a fortune out of dealing with 'the anguish of fame', and parents advised to seek counselling for children doing well at school – because they may be victims of success and suffering from 'over-achiever syndrome'.

True, there are victims in our society. But often of nothing more than the non-fulfilment of expectations. We want and expect to live life with the grit removed, to know things without the discomfort of learning them, and to face only those risks we choose for ourselves. Otherwise, *someone* must be to blame for the falling short.

So many of us think we should have perfect bodies, perfect lifestyles, perfect sex with perfect partners and – if we have spiritual ambitions – perfect understanding, perfect peace of mind, and perfectly wonderful transcendental experiences. A good friend of mine, for example, not noticeably insane, once informed me she intended never to be old, ill or infirm. To that end she was devoting herself to positive thought, regular exercise, and tracking down knowledge about nutrition, complementary medicine, visualisation techniques, and arcane magical thinking. "But you *will* have to die", I said, weakly attempting to introduce a note of reality. "Why?" was the astonishing response. "Because we all do". "Oh yeah, OK, well when I'm about 150 then."

The generalised and unrealistic obsession with perfection, however, in any aspect of life, can only lead to bitterness and disappointment. The idea itself is a wonderful spur; the obsession, and lack of realism, an implacable barrier.

And yet. In times of emergency most of us do rise to the occasion. We summon up our inner resources; we switch our attention away from the ruminating internal focus on what's wrong with our lives, and plug it instead into the immediacy of the world outside; we let go the illusion of control from our minds along with everything that doesn't really matter. And with that letting go comes – we all, I'm sure, have known it – a greatly enhanced capacity to laugh and rejoice in life, and a deeper awareness of and feeling for others. I once heard a former political prisoner, incarcerated on Robben Island for 21 years, saying prison had cured him, very quickly, of any self-pity. And as we know, during World War II the rates of suicide and depression dropped right down.

I am not suggesting that we throw away even an ounce of our hard-won safety and stability. Rather, that we should shift focus and thereby add something. Why wait for a crisis before rising to each occasion and feeling more alive? As a great friend once said to me – isn't every day emergency enough?

27

Staying afloat in the grey and cloudy ocean

THE TIGHTER the tolerance in a component or system, I am informed, the more precise will be its function. Machines with few variations in their tolerance capacity will perform reliably over a precise and narrow range. If for system and component we read society and human individuals, we find that – sadly – in human affairs nothing is very different.

Almost daily we read of people operating within such narrow limits of tolerance that they are virtually perfect machines, wonderfully specialised to behave like medieval zealots. For example, in Northern Nigeria a woman bears a child after a rape and is convicted of adultery, the sentence for which is to be buried in the earth up to her waist and stoned to death. International pressure recently helped free her, but immediately she was released another woman was similarly charged and sentenced. Will the international protest carry over to this new case? Or to the next? And the next? Just as with drugs, we build up a tolerance to outrage.

The pattern of such narrow cruelties recurs many times in different cultures. By contrast, democracies like ours have a wide range of built-in tolerances, enabling a huge variation of people, ideas and behaviours to co-exist. So much so that you could say that British society has a tolerance for change itself – a tolerance which has enabled a huge social revolution to take place over the last 50 years with barely a drop of blood being shed, or anyone quite realising what has happened.

Our personal intolerances, though, are sometimes harder to see. We have our zealots too – particularly focussed on health, food and political correctness – but so far they are not murderers. And we also have unhappy, ineffectual individuals whose tolerances are so tight that they allow no 'play': no space within which their negative emotions and impulses can be contained. So they act them out, sometimes violently. Or, more typically, they internalise the strain and become depressed or anxious.

When such people discover in therapy that it's possible to calm down and tolerate an uncomfortable emotion or idea, they are incredulous. "But it's hard," they complain at first. Meaning: "so I can't do it". Ease and gratification, after all, is what society has trained them for. It comes as a revelation to them that, as psychiatrist Milton Erickson used to say: "it may be hard, but it's not *too* hard". Indeed a wealth of research shows that encouraging someone to express, say, anger ultimately only makes that person more angry.

Many people come into therapy genuinely unaware that they could well be able to tolerate the actions or ideas of others; tolerate failure or hard times; tolerate waiting, and working, for what they want. They have no idea of being a good loser, or taking intelligent risks, or using mistakes as opportunities to learn, or doing anything counter to what they think they are entitled to expect from life. I find myself explaining, usually through metaphor and story, that expectation sets them up for disappointment. And that everything, from the days and the seasons to the fundamental energies of nature itself, all have a wave motion, up and down, nothing is always plain sailing; that to stay afloat on the seas of life we must learn how to keep our experience as manageable as we can, situation by situation. Sometimes all such people need is to understand that they can raise their level of tolerance and so not fear difference or difficulty – and the therapeutic work is done.

As a species, of course, fear is biologically useful: we are pro-grammed to fight, or flee from danger. And perhaps because our society currently has such increasingly broad tolerances that we seem to be trying to fight the fear and risk by refusing to tolerate grey areas. We want everything cut, dried and fixed. For instance, when students in my workshops on therapeutic storytelling realise the power of stories, now and then someone asks: "But can't it be dangerous?" Meaning: "If there's any risk at all, we certainly shouldn't do this".

In my opinion we are disabled and threatened, individually and collectively, by intolerance of the grey – for this is where whatever doesn't fit neatly into our systems can be found; where the hazardous and the confusing and the useful rub shoulders. I remember how a physician friend of my youth treated his terminally ill patients. "Don't worry, Mrs A," he would say, when asked about the anguish ahead. "When the time comes, I won't let you suffer."

I remember one Mrs A, after a bad spell, asking, "has the time come?" And him, smiling and gentle, saying: "no, not yet. But when it does, I'll tell you."

Most doctors were like this at that time, trusted by their patients to free them from life when living became intolerable. It was never easy, because doctors are trained to save life, but it was easier then than now, when the spotlight of analysis and accountability and media scrutiny searches out every grey area. Yet if we light up every square on the board, as currently we try to do, we rule out whatever we can't compute for, like chance, accident, the unforeseen, serendipity, exceptions, luck, and sheer uncategorisable human decency which from time to time needs to fly in the face of the rules.

I have mentioned before in these pages the case of the schoolgirl who, sick of being bottom of the class, cheated in an exam and came top. She liked the feeling, and decided to work for it herself, rather than cheat again and risk being caught. So she did, and found she was clever, and became successful. So what we will not tolerate because it is bad can, in certain instances, be a step towards the good.

It takes tolerance to see the many shades of grey. It is only at the margins of tolerance, wherever we choose to draw the line, that issues become black and white. But the forces of life will not disappear just because we draw a line to exclude them and thus keep them out of awareness. And a society which can't tolerate, or stay afloat in, the grey and cloudy ocean, where it is possible for good (or bad) to be done without any labels, where there are unimaginable options and subtleties and dangers and treasures, is a society trying to rule out of existence anything it fears it cannot control.

Yet life itself will always be bigger than our perceptions and descriptions of it. When we require every issue to fit our rules and preconceptions, then we are fundamentalists too. And that is truly intolerable.

28

A tale of two cultures

CONSIDER TWO CULTURES. The citizens of one regard the emotional storms, mental disruptions, and overwhelming passions that from time to time unbalance them, as visitations from the gods. They believe they are at the mercy of external, supernatural forces; puppets literally driven to distraction by rage, despair and vengefulness, and so are never personally responsible. There is not even a word for 'person' or 'oneself' in their language. They are passive recipients of whatever is hurled at them from the heavens.

The second culture has, with the help of thinkers in the past, decided that man is the measure of all things; that individuality makes for useful diversity; that rationality, restraint and a certain calmness and control (what the Brits used to call the stiff upper lip, in fact) is the most effective way of dealing with mental states that can buffet them about, often so uncomfortably and terribly. They see themselves as captains of their own ships, sailing towards their personal destinies. They are ingenious and creative. And they accept that, given the nature of the world they find themselves in, there will inevitably be short or long periods when they will be battling to navigate their frail craft through choppy waters or violent storms. This they will try and do as best as they can. They do not consider themselves victims.

Time passes. The first culture takes a huge step forward. Philosophers arise who say that human beings are conscious subjects of reflection, responsibility and guilt. What happens to us, they say, can be self-inflicted – by pride, for instance, or ambition, or greed. We may still be torn about by shame, grief or guilt, perhaps, just as we were before – but we have come to understand that this is internally generated, which means that we, rather than the gods, have power over it ourselves, and can address these states and move beyond them. Where before these people spent much of their time placating gods, visiting priests, divining the future and worrying a lot, now they have won some spare capacity. Their culture flourishes.

Meanwhile, the second culture has taken a step backwards. With its capacity for rational and innovative thought, it too has flourished. Living is relatively easy. Nobody starves. People are looked after. They are not at war. But within this apple of desirable existence lurks the worm: nothing requires overwhelming effort any more, because virtually nothing is a matter of survival. The citizens become lazy: fat cats, not much challenged, not much interested in notions of responsibility, capacity and destiny.

Where the first culture turned its attention away from feelings of helplessness, the comfortable citizens of the second turns its attention towards them. With so much time at their disposal, hard won for them by earlier generations, these people now put their attention – with mounting indignation – on whatever mental and emotional pain they may feel.

Specialists in this area replace philosophers, and find a ready audience when they say that unpleasant feelings often arise from a strong emotional reaction to things done to them when young. In other words, it's not their fault. They are victims. And when that happens, their once pragmatic, innovative, cheerfully bloody-minded and individualistic society begins to fall apart.

And now, though you've probably spotted it already, let me identify the two cultures.

The first is archaic Greece – that is to say, before the fifth century BC. In those days, people were probably lucky to last into their thirties, and ripe old age was unlikely, for the fortunate ones, to be more than the mid-fifties. They would have also spent a great deal of their time preoccupied with looking over their shoulders and dodging the wrath of the gods. That, plus their shortish life span, would have left little mental space for anything else.

But then their culture changes its focus. Rational thought and action become a ballast against the blind, destructive force of the passions, and of fate. Through self-knowledge, say their philosophers, reason can analyse and explain human nature, can rule emotion, and can master enslaving appetites. This mental posture frees up creative capacity. Greek civilisation enters its golden age.

The second society – you're probably ahead of me – is us: Western civilisation, inheritors of, among other influences, that glorious

Greek flowering. Of course we all know that cultures and societies and civilisations are dynamic, and can go either backwards and forwards. Nothing remarkable here. But imbued as we are with ideas of progress, we seldom think that *we* could regress. Yet it really seems as if we're currently walking backwards, certainly in Britain, towards a condition analogous to archaic Greece.

The story I've told is a caricature, of course. A kind of cartoon which deliberately skids over facts to catch a pattern spanning these two societies – and then to freeze it for a moment, and see what may be learned. Which is, in my opinion, that we may need to take some more of the medicine which rescued our cultural ancestors, and heed both the Socratic injunction to "know thyself", and Aristotle's dictum that "the unexamined life isn't worth living".

The instinct to know ourselves is, I think, an imperative set deep within us. But the question we seldom ask, because we assume we already know the answer, is whether we actually understand *how* to examine our lives. Indeed in the name of understanding themselves, some people use their intellects to analyse their lives almost out of existence; others endlessly look for reasons why they keep acting against their own best interests, unaware that what passes for 'a reason' is simply plausibility – because given all the forces at work we can seldom know if our explanation is correct. Again, yet others theorise earnestly about the shortfall between what they want and what they get, with little reference to what they need. And all call their processes Knowing Themselves.

Here again, Aristotle can point us in a useful direction, because he also said: "the greatest thing by far is to be a master of metaphor". And it seems to me that what is required is not complex analysis or a hunt for reasons and explanations, but something simpler: a more neutral, more metaphorical, familiarity with one's states of mind, without emotion, bombast or intensity. Perhaps a useful beginning, in fact, is simply to notice that within our consciousness we have literally hundreds of what neurophysiologist Robert Ornstein has called 'small minds'.

It seems to me that these 'small minds' – our resources, knowledge, characteristics, tendencies, qualities, experiences – can be seen as characters who perform in the opera which is our life, going on and off stage according to their roles. But sometimes one character hogs the spotlight and won't stop singing. Anger is onstage, say, when we need Patience or Compassion; Self-pity sings her heart out when the scene is written for Watchful Strength. Anxiety holds up the show, when we need Effective Action. Sometimes, even, a character strays onto our stage singing an aria we've heard before in someone else's opera.

Fortunately, our characters are practised in their roles, and usually appear and disappear on cue, managing the changing situations in our lives more or less smoothly. But if an inappropriate character takes over, and it seems that the plot might be lost, then it is our job as Director of the Opera to step in. For instance: "Kindly leave the stage", we must firmly command Low Spirits. "Optimist – get onstage right now!"

I think we can begin to know something about ourselves by first discovering our own *dramatis personae*. And if we make no judgement beyond whether or not we need any particular character at any particular moment, we may find we can invoke the mind's superb switching mechanism to get it on or off the opera stage quickly, as needed. With practice at so doing we may, with a light heart and lack of self-involvement, gain a measure of control over our own life and work – and thereby become poised to grow and flourish, as the Greeks did.

29

The pleasure in
losing our 'truths'

BACK IN the 1960s, a doctor friend working in medical research told me he'd seen a research paper showing very odd results from a set of double-blind trials – the gold standard of research then as now.

The trials, which had tested a pharmaceutical drug, were repeated every year for nine years, and over that time the results had slowly changed from initially positive to ultimately negative. Fascinated, I asked for the reference. "Well that's the funny thing, dearie," he said, "I've really tried, but just can't seem to find it again".

He was an elderly man, and died a few years later, but over the decades I, too, kept looking for that research. No one remembered it. Perhaps the paper was withdrawn as an 'anomalous reaction', a label researchers give to reliable phenomena (such as the boiling point of water) which on rare and inexplicable occasions don't produce the expected results (which must surely be another phenomenon worth exploring).

And now, half a century later, vindicating a memory I had begun to think I'd imagined, a growing body of research appears to show that indeed all sorts of well-confirmed findings are changing over the years. The phenomenon is called, unofficially, 'the decline effect', and I learned of it from a report by Jonah Lehrer in the *New Yorker* of December 13 2010.

The article's abstract describes it thus: "It's as if our facts are losing their truth: claims that have been enshrined in textbooks are suddenly unprovable ... [and] it's occurring across a wide range of fields, from psychology to ecology."

Among Lehrer's many examples is a recent study of atypical or second-generation antipsychotics, which showed an effect that was less than half of that documented in the first trials in the early nineties. In another example, a paper on the role of 'fluctuating asymmetry' in sexual selection in barn swallows, appeared in Nature in 1991 and was confirmed by about ten independent tests in the following three years.

Then in 1994 the theory started to fall apart. By 1998, of 12 subsequent investigations of fluctuating asymmetry, only a third confirmed the theory, and even those which still gave a positive result also showed a declining effect.

A Stanford epidemiologist, who had looked at the 49 most cited clinical-research studies in three major medical journals, told Lehrer that of those that had been subject to replication, 41% had either been directly contradicted or had their effect sizes significantly downgraded. And of genetic differences in disease risk for men and women "out of 432 claims, only a single one was consistently replicable".

Most scientists I've asked about this are surprisingly unbothered – something I hadn't expected. I even wonder if they are in 'denial' – too uneasy to explore further, even though their explanations may be fair enough. They say that wanting positive results may mean experimenters are not being as accurate as they should be first time round; or they speak of the huge number of variables in the life sciences; or of the perhaps flawed nature of the initial sample to start with; or of the provisional nature of science; or of the trend toward publication of brief one-experiment reports in psychology journals, reporting a single unexpected result, when it used to be a more careful three.

But even so, to me it still seems puzzling. I found myself speculating about 'time' as a factor – something they hadn't mentioned. After all, we know that when people are old or tired, they often 'revert to type'. So perhaps the experiments were getting fatigued? I asked a couple of friendly scientists, and yes, they said, 'reversion to the mean' was a possibility.

Or can experiments 'wear out', I asked, and some (in the softer sciences) faster than others? After all, sand dunes quickly shift their shape in the wind, water needs centuries to wear down boulders, and a molten rock circling the sun and battered over billions of years can change into our verdant planet. So shouldn't time somehow be factored into these experiments? To my surprise, a physicist friend wholeheartedly agreed.

"And when a slice of bread is cut from a loaf", I said, warming to my theme, "it is a different loaf from which another slice is taken the next time. Yet we often look at experimental samples as they exist at a particular moment, as if no 'slices' had ever been cut from them?" My friend allowed this possibility too.

"There is also", I continued, emboldened, "the role of belief. A doctor friend tells me that drugs work for his patients for just as long as he believes in them, and as his belief is strong at the start, he always prescribes new drugs right away."

By now the physicist was giving me funny looks, which grew more so as I babbled on about experimenter effects, and the possibility that time of day – or even date of birth – might have influenced those double-blind results. I could see him regretfully dismissing me as not amusing (which had actually been my intention) and an irrational flake (which had not).

But scientific researchers can be 'irrational' too. For instance, research has now shown that much of what we have discovered about human cognition is dramatically skewed – because seven out of eight people in the world think very differently indeed from the educated Westerners, the majority of them psychology graduates, who comprise a huge 96% of research subjects.

Given that (so far unchallenged) research shows that two-thirds of us are unable to change our minds after receiving new and superior information, will we now modify our reliance on double-blind tests, or on our understanding of human cognition? Or will we simply continue to base our actions, and understanding, on provisional information and flawed trials – or, one might even say, on sophisticated superstition and habit, rather than rationality?

I don't know what effect Lehrer's report will have had on you, but it actually exhilarated me. I'm not, never have been, anti-science, but there is always a sudden moment of delight, relief – and laughter – in finding that things pinned down by measurement or analysis or dogmatic theory have wriggled out of their strait-jackets. Indeed when the illusion of stable reality shifts or cracks, however slightly, it's like a wake-up call. I'm reminded that very little is as cut-and-dried as some scientific popularisers insist; and that there *is* a way out of what we've gone and locked ourselves into.

30

This is the
perfect headline

CERTAINTY is a delicious thing. It's so tempting to want to be sure, to be right – to be beyond criticism and unassailable. Unfortunately anyone thinking like this is usually going doggedly in the wrong direction down a one-way street and about to crash into a brick wall.

Recently I've seen in the therapy room a number of people suffering from ersatz-certainty and the blight of perfectionism. All were talented, capable, likeable people, hard working and conscientious, full of resources and well-intentioned, but each was on the verge of painfully failing at the very thing they set themselves up to be perfect in.

One was trying to work so well that an impossible boss would not be able to humiliate him; another thought that if *she* were good enough that would make her husband stop drinking; another was an entrepreneur for whom failure would mean – he thinks – loss of identity. The illusion of yet another was that only by being unsurpassed in the way she pleased a boyfriend could she 'earn' love and friendship.

Every criticism, every niggle or pinprick, from boss, lover, authority figure or friend caused these people to feel they had no value. In a phrase they all used, at such times the ground disappeared beneath their feet.

I am reminded of the memorable time when I joked with a high-achieving friend for whom no man ever seemed good enough. Was she waiting for John the Baptist? I asked. She took this as a wounding insult. Why, she replied without a trace of humour, had I not said Jesus Christ? This intelligent and sensitive woman seriously thought 'being worth it' could be demonstrated by the perfection of the man who chose her to marry him.

I remember, too, the puzzled unhappiness of a woman whose competence in many departments of life was truly intimidating. She had organised a 'perfect' party for her sister's birthday, invited her sister's friends (of whom I was one), cooked a superb meal, provided a gracious environment, and had been genuinely appreciated and thanked for all of it. But as the guests bantered and basked in the warmth and friendship generated that evening, the hostess was unable to join in. I could see her thinking: "I made all this possible. What more should I have done to make me one of them?"

In the novel *Sentimental Tommy*, by J.M. Barrie, the orphan Tommy is given the chance to enter an essay competition to be written in the formal Scottish language, for which the prize is a university bursary. If he fails, he'll have to go to "the herding": become a shepherd or cowman. Tommy is bright, intelligent and quick-witted, well capable of winning the scholarship. But at one point a word he wants eludes him. Instead of finding a way round the problem, he spends the rest of the allotted time searching his mind vainly for the precise word (a 'hantle') and fails to complete the paper.

As ever, once the exam was over and the pressure off, the word came flying back into his mind. But in his obsession to find the perfect word in the allotted time, Tommy lost his chance of further education.

Perfectionists are always like this: pointing the wrong way, eyes focussed on putting themselves beyond criticism by the consistent correctness and superiority of everything they do. But the solution usually lies in the polar opposite direction – in admitting that we are all flawed people in a flawed world. After all, no one can be perfect unless they can admit to their faults, and if they admit to their faults, how can they be perfect? "Bachelors' wives and old maids' children are always perfect", as the saying goes.

Most perfectionists I have come across, myself included when I get like that, transpose what should be inward for the view from outside – as did my clients, my high-achieving friend, and the woman at the birthday party. They substitute performance for authentic behaviour, sacrificing realism, allowing their own voice to be muffled and their own path obscured. Or, like Tommy, they do the reverse, focussing so exclusively on an inward drive for perfection that there is a gaping mismatch between the effort within and the world outside.

Contrary to the conventional view, perfectionism's basis seems not so much poor self-image as inflated self-love, otherwise known as Pride, said in the Bible to be the worst of the Seven Deadly Sins.

When I was young this mystified me. But later I understood that when puffed up with pride one simply couldn't *learn* anything. Other of the Deadly Sins, such as Greed, Sloth, or Lust, for example, are recognisable as part of oneself, and so can be addressed. But pride masquerades as the whole person. It is too global, too all-encompassing, harder to spot, harder to admit.

Defending the edifice built on the need for perfection is exhausting, of course, because it is impossible, and in the process perfectionists become the perfect mark for the bully. Yet even a blunt but well-intentioned confrontation can breach those defences as powerfully as any maliciously aimed criticism or taunt, and slash deep into an already festering wound.

Perfectionists are very aware of status and pecking orders, and their place in them. But life is much easier (and not only for perfectionists) if we loosen the bonds of hierarchy to some extent, and join the crowd jogging along somewhere in the middle. And easier still when we learn not to mind being a fool. Then when we slip on any of life's banana skins, there is nothing we have to defend. We can simply pick ourselves up and say: 'I'm such an idiot. Now what can I learn from what happened?"

I remember the wonder of realising, as a child, that something could be dry only because wet existed; that the fact that I felt hunger meant that food must exist; that if any need or state existed, that implied the existence of its answering condition. That childhood perception holds, and tells me that if we yearn for the perfect, then perfection must indeed exist. But in order to approach it we may need less effort than perfectionism demands, but in another direction: something humbler, closer to simplicity.

Probably most of us have perfectionist moments, at certain times in certain departments. But context, as usual, is crucial. Had Tommy been writing something for its own sake, for the love of it, with no outcome or judgement by others contingent on the result, his search for the exact word would not have harmed him. All creative artists are, I think, perfectionists – seeking at their own pace to speak with their own voice. I think, too, that whenever appropriate, such focussed aspiration towards perfection applies equally well to the art of living.

31

Hello... is anyone in there?

MY OLD FRIEND Mireille and I were chatting about the pregnancy of our mutual friend Sheila. Her five-year-old daughter overheard us. "Sheila's having a baby!" she exclaimed. "Who is ... um ... I think .... who is ... er ... who ...?" She struggled, reaching through the terrestrial warp for words that would match what she saw in her mind. After much furrowing of her brow, she found them and burst out: "Who is she getting for a baby?"

It has taken decades to work through the either/or thinking in the nature-nurture debate to reach the point we could have started from – that there is an interplay between heredity and environment. But in her simplicity that five-year-old expressed something I think essential in this regard and too often unconsidered – who, exactly, is it that the genetic inheritance and the environment are acting upon? Or even – who did our parents get for a baby?

Suggesting a ghost in the machine in this way upsets reductionists, I know. "This 'who' you speak of" I hear them say, "does it have substance? How do you test for it? Can you measure it?" I have no answer, except to say that neither can I measure my love for my grandchildren or my gratitude for the beauty of a rose. And that without the concept of the 'who' inside us, upon whom the conditioning and inherited tendencies act, we can justifiably wonder whether we exist at all. More useful, I think, to bypass debate and see this idea as metaphorical rather than metaphysical – recognising, of course, that metaphor's power goes way beyond mere poetic ornament.

I remember a friend elaborating, as clearly he had many times before, on the many horrors his mother had inflicted on him, cataloguing instances of her ability to wound, her inability to love. "What did *you* do?", I asked. "How did *you* respond?" His focus shifted immediately, as if he'd woken from a dream. Until that moment, he had been invisible to himself in respect of these memories. Now he remembered himself as himself, from within himself, and being reminded of himself, was no longer his mother's victim.

I think the contention that the 'who' within us indeed exists, even if deeply buried, is so useful, because living 'as if' it exists supplies a focus which is both energising and optimistic. For instance, a client of mine (she'd had years of psychoanalysis) told me repeatedly that she understood absolutely everything about herself. She also prided herself on never fearing confrontation, always speaking her mind, and forever being ready to "tell the truth" and put people straight. Consequently she gave pain to others (which she hardly noticed) and frequently found herself deliberately shunned (which she hated).

She was convinced she had no option but to be forthright and outspoken because, as she emphatically told me: "this is who I am." Adding, self-righteously: "And it is also my ethics." Her tone of voice brooked no argument.

But it took fewer than ten minutes to establish that her mother had been timid and diplomatic, and that as a child my client decided she didn't want to be like that. Instead, she would always jump in or speak out – a decision that still ruled her, but coded into her as a compulsion by now, not choice. That decision closed out the development of other capacities she needed – such as restraint, to name but one. What was required now was to step back from the notion that her dominant characteristic – confrontation – was 'who she was' and connect instead to the idea that the 'who' inside her was making a journey through life, and could learn from the feedback of each experience as she went through it.

Although she had held such a limiting view of herself for more than 50 years, and suffered the tangle of consequences, she quickly came to see that 'who she was' was certainly bigger than a few threads of behaviour which kept her many resources hidden from her. Indeed, as soon as she realised that she was *somebody*, and always had been, she quickly moved forward psychologically. And the possibility was also opened up that one day she might even recognise and remember the 'who' within.

In my opinion, this is what the 'insight therapies' miss. Like my client herself, they are full of plausible-enough insights within the theory of the therapy, but shine little or no light on the fact that once needs are met and cognitive, emotional and behavioural management is improved, space opens up in the mind, and with this the possibility of increased autonomy for the 'who', the core individual, within.

There was another friend, too, who during a long nervous breakdown had tried to set fire to her apartment. One day, as she sat babbling wild rubbish, I said: "Mary, listen. I want to talk to the sane part of you. Please call her." Mary nodded, and straightened up like a good little girl, some clarity returning to her eyes – a look from the 'who' within, perhaps. At which point it was possible to have a conversation and reach an agreement that the 'sane part' would be watchful and keep Mary safe.

Aha, some might say, that's just the superego you called on! And others: it was merely conscience! Yes, perhaps, if one remembers that in French the word conscience also means 'consciousness'. But for practical purposes it is more helpful to regard the 'who' within us as an essential awareness which transcends the many aspects of personality, and which remains the same, whether we are two, or twelve, or 32, or 72 – or even my own great age!

And it is there even when the body is damaged, and movement and speech all but disappear. In this respect Stephen Hawking has given this culture more than a view of the universe and the nature of time – he is in himself a visible symbol of a mind flying high above the ruined castle of its body.

And it is there too, I think, though it cannot show itself, when the brain is damaged, as in dementia. Then the 'who' inside seems, to those of us on the outside, like a driver knocked unconscious in a car careering out of control. But I have always found communication possible with dementing people, though through story and metaphor rather than facts. And people also seem able to communicate in some way with individuals apparently 'absent' – stroke victims, people in a coma, people dying. They simply tune their awareness to the 'who'-ness of the other, and feel the contact to be real.

How is it that the child I quoted at the start saw what is hard for so many adults to acknowledge, even as metaphor? Let me end as I started, with a child's view. An eight-year-old friend asked me about a book I was reading for review. I told him it was about the illusions and mistakes that people are prone to, which stop them thinking straight. Meeting his open gaze, I added: "But this doesn't usually apply to children. They often think more clearly than grown-ups." As he considered this he became very quiet. Then he replied: "Yes that's true. We kids don't know enough to fool ourselves".

32

A matter
of form

"THE U.S. standard railroad gauge is 4 feet, 8.5 inches", writes Professor Tom O'Hare, of the University of Texas, in *How Specs Live Forever*, which has been circulating on and off the Web since 1996. I've referred to this before, but it bears repeating from a different perspective.

O'Hare asks: " ... Why was that gauge used? Because that's the way they built them in England, and the US railroads were built by English expatriates.

"Why did the English people build them like that? Because the first rail lines were built by the same people who built the pre-railroad tramways, and that's the gauge they used.

"Why did they use that gauge then? Because the people who built the tramways used the same jigs and tools they used for building wagons, which used that wheel spacing. ..."

Step by step, O'Hare methodically tracks the gauge's history back to the ancient Romans, and reveals that our railway gauge is based on a form created more than two millennia ago and carried down unaltered through the centuries. Indeed an engineer I know claims to have since found exactly the same gauge associated with spacecraft.

O'Hare's observations seem to me the perfect metaphor for a persistent condition in human life – the need for ideas and intentions to find containers for their expression, and the fact that new content will almost always drop into existing forms.

This must be why, when an artist or writer or composer manages to create a new form, there's an outpouring from others adopting it for their own creative impulses and ideas, and new 'schools' of painting, poetry or music are born.

And this is probably why at one point, as Bishop Tutu had warned them, the once noble African National Congress began to seem in some ways like the government it once fought to overcome – trapped increasingly within the very form it opposed while struggling for liberation.

And it may also explain why the ordinary Russian people, more often than not dominated and oppressed over the centuries by despotic Czars, found that after the 1914 – 18 revolution they ended up with very similar forms of subjection. But now, however, instead of Czars, they were dominated by equally despotic 'Commie Czars'.

Anthropologists have shown that when attempts are made to superimpose patterns of thought on a population's traditional beliefs, the new ideas are often hijacked by the pre-existing form. Missionaries bringing 'the word of the Lord' to a tribe in Papua New Guinea, say, may find that though the message has been enthusiastically received, in practice the newly adopted belief soon turns back, in all but name, into a version of what was there before.

Sometimes, even the missionary's own beliefs topple into those of the host tribe. Daniel Everett, author of *Don't sleep, there are snakes*, lost his Christian faith after many years spent with the Amazonian Piraha Indians, and himself took on the precise view of life he had arrived to convert the tribe away from. His description of that process is as painful as it is hilarious, and in my opinion should be required reading for everyone interested in the transmission of human ideas.

It seems to me too that a spectacular example of form swallowing content is currently happening in front of our eyes. As Christopher Booker pointed out in *The Neophiliacs*, between the mid-1950s and 1960s a bloodless, almost wordless, social revolution came to a head and transformed the British into a classless society. The majority of citizens were no longer the toiling serfs of earlier centuries. And those at the top, a significant proportion of whom had through privilege become snobbish, amoral twits, could no longer think themselves masters of the universe.

You can probably see where I'm going with this: in spite of our rhetoric of equality, a new group has taken on the forms those aristocratic predecessors vacated. A significant proportion of bankers and politicians are now displaying in their behaviour, if not their words, an identical contempt for those 'beneath' them. The acquisition of wealth and social position has not brought out the best in them.

Form is obviously essential on this planet, but all too often, like an invisible black hole, it gobbles up whatever content falls into it. Bertold Brecht describes a character, Mr Keuner, who once worked for a gardener. Keuner was told to trim a laurel tree standing in a pot. The tree was hired out for celebrations, and had to be spherical. Keuner began pruning the trailing shoots, but no matter how hard he tried, found himself lopping off too much on one side, then too much on the other. When the tree was at last spherical, it was also very small. The gardener said: "Good! That's the sphere, but where's the laurel?"

Forms can at best, I think, be valuable, or else expedient, anchors. But they can also become balls and chains that weigh us down, particularly when we are apprehensive, preoccupied, old, or tired. That is when we tend to do as plants do, and 'revert to type', by collapsing back into forms we thought we'd left behind. In fact the 'standard human product' seems ultimately to be fodder for pre-existing forms.

The way out of this prison, or so it seems to me, is to accept that willy-nilly we live inside it most of the time – but that we need to be able to break out when necessary. This is what exceptional people do so deftly. For example, my Dutch-born friend Fieke, a small and very beautiful woman, was once visiting a sick friend in an African township in Johannesburg (an illegal and dangerous act in those apartheid days). With no road width to get closer, she parked her car on wasteland at the township's edge. After her visit, when she was back in the car and leaving to return home, three seriously large thugs appeared. Two rocked her car from the back and the third, spanner in hand, crawled across the bonnet towards the windscreen. Fieke did not fall into available forms of fear or anger. Instead she did the unexpected. She very sweetly blew the men kisses. That so destabilised them that she was able to get away.

From time to time, particularly in emergencies, we all find ourselves doing the unexpected. And I imagine we all tend to treasure and tell stories about such events, just as I treasure and tell many stories about my friend Fieke, as close as a sister to me, who died a few weeks ago, as cleanly as she had lived. So perhaps one can deduce that the way to escape the imprisoning forms would be to treat every day as an emergency.

33

Letting go needs
no time at all

THERE ARE times in life when most of us hang on so grimly to what we don't need – memories, material things – that our houses, our possessions, and our minds become warehouses of the past rather than workshops of the present. Memories and associations lie quite forgotten, like thick dust in an abandoned house, inert until we stir them up with our attention. At which point, while *remembering* is perfectly comfortable, *reliving* so entangles us in the past that it seems inconceivable that we could ever let it go.

Recently I sat with a box of old photographs meaning to discard most of them, and finding it almost impossible to discard any. Mostly I was drawn into a trance of happy or nostalgic, memories. But even those few which reminded me of unhappiness, though more easily chucked, often had some saving grace, even if only the artistic merit of the picture itself. And when it didn't, I'd sometimes even tell myself I'd send the picture to the person depicted – "they'll like that". The subtext of which was "and then *they* can throw it away".

Of course I'm not the only one. One of my therapy clients had lived for years surrounded by packing cases, unable to unpack or discard them yet constantly troubled by their presence. Another client hoarded old grievances and, injustices, which would erupt again and again whenever he encountered vaguely similar circumstances. Their lives were so stuck that nothing had happened for years, nor was likely to, until they could free up some mental space and energy.

At first, though they wanted to, neither could conceive of *how* to let their lumber go; both had the same paralysing idea that they would need to look at every individual item again, to be *quite* sure they could find no reason to keep it. Like slaves restrained by their masters' chains, they were shackled by the visual evidence of the past. But imagine one's master being a box of photographs, a packing case, a memory.

Years ago I coined an aphorism: "You can live your life or you can relive your life – but you sure can't do both at the same time." By saying that I was trying to free clients from the notion that poring over the past was enough to move them forward in the present. But I think my comment had wider relevance, because to be entranced by the past under *any* circumstances actually robs one of the present.

The traffic goes in both directions too. Sometimes I observe a younger version of a client invade the here-and-now, valiantly taking on tasks for which no child is equipped. For example, in certain kinds of adult confrontation, a five-year-old may pop up unbidden, determined to handle the situation, turning the adult they have since become into a sudden, helpless jelly. Or a traumatised toddler will charge out of the mists with tumultuous energy, responding again, and again and again, to something that happened years before. If a child felt a parent's behaviour as deeply unjust, for instance, it will jostle the adult aside *whenever* injustice is perceived, reacting to every unjust incident with the same off-the-scale level of fury and indignation. The adult they have become would probably be well equipped to assess and handle these various situations – but it's the child who gets there first.

Almost daily we can notice the past invading the present, or the present drowning in the past. Wars are fought for ancient causes. Trouble in families goes right back to childhood envies. A man is driven down a pointless path in life to settle a frustrated hope born decades earlier. Traditions evolve and are treasured, commemorating forgotten events that happened centuries before.

Equally, of course, the future can invade the present. I know a playwright who begins work in the morning, but soon is lost in powerful daydreams in which he is acknowledging the tumultuous applause on opening night. Another individual, (and sometimes, in the past it was me), will put their attention on an anticipated event – a meeting, say, or a party – and is so consumed by the promise it holds that the rest of the week passes by in a blur. While yet others cringe from a future juggernaut of retribution for a mistake that most people would easily handle. What are we to make of this muddle? How to pick our way through the maze of disorder, debris, and pleasure gardens littering the past and future?

Physicists have found, as they go deeper into matter, that at the subatomic level time ceases to exist. The same thing happens to us, of course — time disappears as we travel deeper within ourselves. This timeless, shadowless interior place is the workshop where much that hitherto has bound and confined us can be resolved, expanded, understood, or overwritten. It is where the best therapeutic work is done, and also where great creative minds find their riches. And it is where we can easily let go of past or future physical or mental clutter, thus making room in the present for movement and change – and for opportunities to present themselves.

Our innate capacity to jump around in time and space is a glorious gift – one we use to solve problems, make discoveries, create art, and explore beyond the walled city of day-to-day consciousness. We use it whenever we hear a story and suddenly find ourselves long ago and far away. I have read of a small boy who, on the verge of violent seasickness, was promptly told a story by his resourceful mother and instead of heaving and retching, he found himself swept down the centuries into a fantastic adventure in medieval Japan. What a gift, with a split-second switch of attention, to travel on the magic carpet of the mind through time and space, and share in the brilliant world of "cloud-capped towers and gorgeous palaces".

Recently a *New Scientist* article speculated about the possibility of time travel. *But we have time travel already!* We use it so often and so naturally that we barely notice or appreciate it. Yet if we are prepared to be open-minded, and travel light, we may encounter in our wayfaring endless, astonishing bounty and marvels. Sometimes, like tourists everywhere, we can even bring back remarkable gifts. The pity of it, however, is that so often we visit, and revisit, places that have so little to offer.

34

How to make friends
across time

WHILE TALKING to a sparky and immensely likeable 18-year-old about the politics essay he was writing, I recommended certain books he might usefully consult. "No I don't do books", he said airily. "There's loads of stuff on the Web I can pinch".

Well I've done that too. We all have. When something we want is unprotected and in front of our eyes, it's an open invitation to 'pinch' it. But the casualness with which this young man talked about nicking material, (or 'plagiarism', as it is politely known), his sense of entitlement, and his lack of understanding of the value of books, saddened me. For the truth is, we are lucky to have both Web and book.

The Web, that cornucopia of ideas and materials accessed at lightning speed, lets us switch from one associated source to the next, seeking what we want, seeing what's out there, getting hold of it. This is nothing like the almost palpable interaction between book and reader, the slowing down and relaxed inwardness. We tend to become speedy when sourcing information on the Web, perhaps because the screen is so sterile and impermeable. What we find on it has no physical existence, and disappears in a flash. A book may become a friend. A file or 'doc', on the other hand, will not.

Indeed, we can have long-term, almost physical, relationships with books – or rather, with those books whose impact or impression has lodged in us. Once they absorb us we grow quiet, steadied and thoughtful. Their look, their feel, their smell, their dimension and weight, engage us. Memories, and moods and ideas adhere to them (admittedly not always beneficially).

But whether from book or Web, appropriating materials can be theft – of potential income for a living author, and also of intellectual property. Some of the 'stuff' my young friend was so easily transferring to his essay would have demanded effort, sweat and sacrifice to create. It takes time and sustained energy to find new ideas and express them with style and clarity – and while all that is going on the bills still have to be paid.

It would be fair enough, perhaps, if the author of the source material were long dead. But the living really should be able to earn from those who 'employ' the fruits of their work, and so should their families for a while thereafter, given that they would have missed out on those earnings while the author, whether parent or spouse, was toiling away. This is the basis of copyright law. But here we are, like feudal lords, myself included even though I claim to know better, unthinkingly treating their work as ours by right, enabled by the fact that since the advent of the photocopier the whole idea of copyright has been gradually eviscerated by technology.

This is not the first time a new 'technology' has threatened the natural right of authors to their work. After shorthand was invented, for instance, reporters hired by a rival theatre producer could attend a new Elizabethan play and take down the whole script practically verbatim. There was no checking for accuracy, no protection, no concept of acknowledgement, no 'rights'.

Until recently, too, ideas generated by women were unprotected, unrecognised, and likely to be appropriated by their men. The scientific contribution of Ada Lovelace, for example, was only recently properly appreciated. Dorothy Wordsworth saw the field of daffodils, described the experience in her journal, noted how they "tossed & reeled & danced" – and then her brother William wrote the famous poem.

Again, French writer Colette's husband Willi passed off her novels as his own. Microbiologist Rosalind Franklin was virtually airbrushed out of the Nobel prize-winning papers on the double-helix, though her work was crucial to the breakthrough. And Jocelyn Bell Burnell, who in 1968 first discovered quasars, was later similarly excluded from the Nobel Prize by her senior (male) colleagues.

But why am I so exercised by all of this? It's obvious why the theft from women is objectionable, but pinching ideas from Web or book? Surely that isn't the same?

Well in an essential way I think it is – because these examples illuminate how, in all life's departments, we tend to skim over the surfaces, joining up the dots of current convention and practice to make the picture that suits us, ignorant or unaware of the texture and depths and connections and history and human effort that lie underneath those surfaces. This makes us shallow, and our behaviour – in the long run – dangerous, sometimes because the information is just wrong, but most of all because it restricts our experience, and consequently our perception and judgement.

Certain individuals will grow and deepen, of course, as I'm confident my young essay-writing friend will do. I hope he will become aware, for example, that behind the evolution of the computer lies the effort of many minds, including that of Ada Lovelace and all the others who over several centuries invented or foresaw the relevant machines and processes, or took forward the necessary theories and concepts. In an analogous way, behind the making of a book lies not only the toil of the author but the development of our alphabet, the machines involved, the trees from which the paper was made, and the work of the originators of every process through which that book arrives in our hand. And behind both, as behind everything, is the primary essential – the transmission of ideas.

It seems to me that appropriating ideas, without digestion or a moment's gratitude or acknowledgement, is what constitutes the theft. Copyright is a necessary 'policeman'. But way beyond that, something far more personal is required: we need to regenerate any idea from scratch, and put it in such new language that it really is our own.

By re-presenting it in fresh words, giving it context and room to breathe (plus ample dollops of acknowledgement), we avoid diluting an idea or reducing it to a slogan. Then it's no longer a question of 'ownership', but of participation. And it is one of life's greatest delights to discover within an idea those other earlier minds which have already, or originally, formulated it in their own words, for their own time and possibly for all time.

As Emerson put it: "All my best thoughts were stolen by the ancients". That, it seems to me, is the right way round – the point of view which creates enduring friendships across time.

35

The button that holds it together

MANY YEARS ago I was hired to write a feature film from a novel by Brigid Brophy. I saw my task to be as faithful to her book as possible, but the producer set me right. "Forget the book", he said in his languid Texan drawl, "I bought a button. Your job is to sew a pair of pants round it".

I asked why he'd bothered about the book at all, in that case, and he explained that he liked something about the central idea, and bought the rights to avoid being sued. In fact he'd also bought rights to another novel, in some ways similar, just to be safe.

All this came back to me after watching *The Thirty-Nine Steps* on TV recently. The book by John Buchan, written in 1915, is a gripping adventure story set just before the outbreak of World War I, in which a courageous hero faces extreme dangers to keep vital British military secrets safe from villainous German spies. There are few women in the story, and no love interest. In this recent version, however, the hero is rather wet, and often saved from disaster only by the intrepid heroine – a suffragette with a photographic memory, knowledge of chemistry and karate, who is also an undercover member of MI5. By the story's end they are, of course they are, in love.

There have been at least six versions of *The Thirty-Nine Steps* over the years. Film-makers seem much taken with the essential story – innocent patriot on the run, in fear for his life, hunted down by his own side as well as by the enemy – yet every version departs from it substantially. Even the '39 steps' themselves, where they are and what they are, vary from film to film, all differing from the book and from each other. But the button, the core story, is always recognisable.

Well, such distortions happen, and perhaps it doesn't matter, except to some (though not all) authors. It's only fiction, after all.

But unfortunately the film world treats history in the same way. 'Braveheart', I read, was not a commoner clawing his way up from the bottom to defend his homeland but, in the film, a knight from a noble family. His father wasn't killed by the English, but fought for them in exchange for political favour. And among the BBC's many inventions in *The Tudors* series, Henry VIII had two sisters not one, and the sister whom the film dispensed with was actually the one who went to France (not Portugal) to marry the ageing king she did not in fact murder.

And so on and so on. The Americans did not crack the Enigma code, as we are told in a film (though neither would the British have done so without the pioneer work of the Poles, who are also dropped from the story). And if you saw the rough, inquisitorial interviews in the film *Frost/Nixon*, it's worth knowing that in reality these two men had a business deal whereby Nixon got 20 percent of the proceeds from the interviews. So they were partners, not antagonists, and Nixon knew he had to deliver a dramatic revelation if the interviews were to make good money.

Film-makers say their work is 'just entertainment', that they must alter the facts to make a story that works, and that if we want to know the truth we can go to the history books. However these days the majority of people get their knowledge of historical events from films, TV, and fiction, or the shifting texts of Wikipedia, rather than from what are deemed more reliable sources.

And even so, of course, history is simply what some people think happened. Historians do their best, but their work is inevitably loaded with bias, distortion and confusion. For example we assume Napoleon was small only because of confusion between old French feet and Imperial (British) feet. When measured shortly after his death, Napoleon was recorded at 5ft 2in in French feet, which is 5ft 6½ in Imperial feet, which was slightly taller than the average Frenchman of his day. His nickname, '*le petit caporal*', perpetuated that rumour – because non-francophones assumed that '*petit*' referred to his height. But it was a term of affection, based on his camaraderie with ordinary soldiers.

I have a taste for this kind of debunking, but how do I know if even the foregoing (I read it on the Web) is true? And the further back in time we go the dimmer the view becomes, the more invisible the button, and the more ornamental and capacious the pants. Was there ever a historical Jesus? What are the real facts of Gautama Buddha's life? What was the real function of the Pyramids?

But then, are we ever aware, even in our lifetimes, of what may have happened even in our own families? The father of a friend of mine, a respectable businessman and a pillar of society, was in his youth imprisoned for fraud – and his son, an eminent lawyer went to his grave never knowing that. None of those who knew, myself included, ever told him.

Yet in spite of artefacts, fantasy and special pleading – the pleats, folds and tucks in the capacious pants, so to speak – there's always a button holding the story together. Here are the bones of a simple tale with a repetitive refrain, (no space for all of it), which provides an apt metaphor:

"There once was a tailor, who made clothes for other people in his village, and who longed for a fine coat of his own. So whenever he finished a job he kept the leftover cloth, however small, and when there was enough he patched the pieces into a coat. He loved that coat, and wore it whenever he could. In fact he wore it and wore it – until it was all worn out."

"At least he thought it was all worn out, but when he looked he saw that by judicious cutting and patching, he could turn the coat into a jacket, and this he did. And he wore it and wore it until it was all worn out."

"At least he thought it was all worn out, but when he looked again he saw that by clever cutting and stitching, he could turn the jacket into a waistcoat, and this he did. And he wore it and wore it until it was all worn out."

And so the story goes. To the accompanying refrain, the waistcoat wears out and is turned into a vest, and then the vest into a cap. Finally there is just enough cloth left to cover a button.

"And he wore that button on his favourite shirt, and wore it and wore it until it was all worn out."

"At least he thought it was all worn out, but when he looked again, he saw there was just enough ... *to make this story*."

The cloth wears out. The button lasts longer. And even when all events are forgotten, the story remains. I'm often reminded of this, when people come to me for their first psychotherapeutic session. Very often they try to describe their troubled history and lose themselves in elaborate, unstoppable details. At such times it is crucial to disconnect one's gaze from the embroidered fabric – and focus on the button which holds it all together.

And that puts me in mind of Sir Geoffrey Jackson, Britain's Ambassador to Uruguay, who was kidnapped in 1971 by the Tupamaros guerrillas, and imprisoned, alone, in a cramped man-made 'hole' underground for eight months. Later I heard him talk about the experience. He had kept his mental balance, he said, by conscious exercise of body and mind. One such exercise he devised, he said, was "trawling for gold" – reviewing in his mind the events of what he thought was a day (without daylight he couldn't ever be sure), and collecting every moment, however brief, that was in some way positive or valuable.

What he did was to me an object lesson – the very reverse of what film-makers and historians tend to do. Geoffrey Jackson deliberately discarded the unnecessary fabric of every single day, and held on instead to all the golden buttons.

36

Eureka moments? It may depend on little coot

MY HIGH-FLYING friend Elise is an energetic and unusual woman with a gift for success, something of a polymath but mainly a novelist. More than once she has told me how she keeps hunting for 'the real thing' – the big idea through which she will make her contribution, by writing something which might make an impact, perhaps over centuries. She cudgels her brains, but has never found her theme. Nothing seems weighty or important enough.

She mentioned this again recently, and a story jumped into my mind which matched and mirrored – and also offered a solution to – her quest. Moreover, it is about the act of creation itself, and it has lasted over centuries.

It is part of the creation myth of the Cheyenne Indians, in North America, and begins at a time when the world has not yet come into being. All that exists is water, and above it, sky and clear air, inhabited by the only life yet possible, that of the birds. The birds know that earth lies beneath the water, and that the task is to bring it up into the air. They feel the stirring of creation moving in them, and the high flyers, three great birds, offer to fly high and then dive down as deep as they can, to get the earth up.

I create the scene in my imagination. First, Grand Eagle summons up his strength, and dives deep. But he comes up with nothing. Then Great Auk, an excellent swimmer, who can bank, veer and turn under the water, plunges in and swims down, but to no avail. Then Mighty Guan, who today lives only on top of extinct volcanoes in remote cloud forests, makes the attempt, but comes up with nothing.

And then, the story relates, after a pause, and from a different direction altogether, along comes 'little Coot', hardly the most impressive or high-ranking of birds, sculling along the surface of the water. He is a diver too. None of the big birds take much notice of him. But down he goes, and he is the one who finally comes up with a little bit of mud in his beak – the beginnings of our earth, and source of everything that will come into being.

And there it is, metaphors and patterns laid out for one tribe, centuries ago and (at this simple level and in this specific facet of a much more complex story) very easy to 'read'. High flying ideas will not be anywhere near as useful to Elise as the unassuming dive of the humble coot. A bit of unformed mud brought up from the depths of her own imagination is all she needs to begin bringing her work into durable form – plus, of course, luck and inherent capacity.

Although I do not possess Elise's determined ambition, I find (as I'm sure we all do) that the way I enter my creative imagination is often decidedly coot-like. Bountiful ideas, I've noticed, can at first seem insignificant. Softly, lightly, they edge themselves across the outer horizon of consciousness when the mind is idling, unclouded by ambition or desire or anything else. If one has any expectation of a dazzling 'eureka' moment, then what floats up to the surface, quietly and unobtrusively, would be easy to miss. The signal is usually so subtle it is hardly there at all.

This brings me to the work of a physicist friend researching into 'creativity' and currently looking for famous 'eureka' moments. He has numerous examples from the sciences, but so far only one from the arts – Paul McCartney waking up one morning singing 'scrambled eggs' to the tune of what became *Yesterday*. And he wonders if the relatively rare examples from the humanities (if this really is true) betokens a fundamental difference in thinking between artist and scientist.

But it seems to me that artists and scientists have different objectives, methods and strategies, and seek very different types of solutions. Artists' equivalents of 'eureka moments' are often lengthy, sustained, even mediumistic episodes – because the 'unformed mud' may need to be rendered into a complete 'world' before it dries up or dissolves. This may be why my friend hasn't found them. Stevenson, for example, wrote *Dr Jekyll and Mr Hyde* in a weekend. Coleridge's *Kubla Khan* poured out of him after an opium dream – until his mind was wrenched back to the mundane world by the door bell.

And most extraordinary of all, Rainer Maria Rilke created a masterpiece of German literature and a landmark of modern poetry at near-inhuman speed – 55 profound and utterly extraordinary *Sonnets to Orpheus* in 13 days. He described the process as "the most enigmatic dictation I have ever received: the whole first part was taken down in a single breathless act of obedience, between the 2nd and 15th of February 1922, without one word being in doubt or having to be changed." Then immediately afterwards, equally precipitately, a totally unexpected bonus poured out – the extraordinary, transcendent *Duino Elegies*.

But whether they arrive as a eureka moment or a longer episode, inspiring ideas seem to come to great artists and scientists alike in the lightness of dreams, images, metaphors, and flashes of understanding – gifts from the deep, so to speak, from 'little Coot'. And most often they seem to arrive, again equally, after a period of confusion, depression, despair, or madness almost – much diving down, in fact, and coming up with nothing.

But then comes the divergence. Work in the arts is intensely private, not to be shown to others, or much spoken of, before completion – because doing so will cause the spring to leak away. In the sciences, however, discussion and exchange of ideas is essential. Indeed, others may quite openly be working on the identical problem.

Finished work, too, is intensely emotional and utterly individual in the arts – and retains those qualities over time. The scientist, however, transforms the 'eureka' flash into an unemotional, formal and detached report.

What is more, as cell biologist Lewis Wolpert has pointed out, "one measure of the significance of a scientific paper is how many other papers it makes irrelevant." Wolpert knows whereof he speaks: he tells me he had two, if not three, 'eureka moments' during his breakthrough research into how living cells behave during embryonic development.

But a scientific breakthrough is never the sole property of that scientist. Ultimately, in Wolpert's words, "the solution will be assimilated into the body of scientific knowledge, superseding what has gone before". In the arts, however, what came earlier remains valid. Wagner's operas did not make Mozart's irrelevant, nor Shakespeare render Chaucer obsolete.

But whether art or science, and however differently 'eureka moments' manifest, they always depend on what is brought from the depths. My friend Elise is still focused on the great, high flying birds. In my opinion, she'd be better off waiting for little Coot – but only if she is tenacious and has already done the necessary work. Pasteur nailed it when he wrote: "Fortune favours the prepared mind."

37

Bringing it all together

I HAVE BEEN brooding about the phenomenon of focus, both internal and outward, and there seems to me little difference between the two. For instance when our attention is focussed on a heartfelt personal question or quandary, that is to say when we are genuinely seeking some sort of 'answer', then that answer will often arrive by way of a dream. Or sometimes the world itself will provide the answer by presenting a sequence of events quite oddly, in a metaphorical, dream-like way.

In a letter to a friend, the late poet Ted Hughes describes going down to a pond where he used to catch pike. The lodge was a ruin and the garden a forest. The pond had shrunk to an oily puddle "about twenty feet across in a black basin of mud, with oil cans and rubbish". His son made a few casts into the poisoned looking water among the rubbish. "It was horrible, and depressing," wrote Hughes. "My name carved on the trees." It began to pour with rain. He made "one token cast – a ceremonial farewell – and there among the rubbish I hooked a huge perch. The biggest I ever caught."

The metaphorical resonances are obvious. I am reminded of a day in my own life when a question that wouldn't leave me alone – what lessons could I learn from my specific family history? – was answered by an extraordinary sequence of strange, surrealistic events, one after another, too many and too long to detail here. For a period of twelve hours a series of connected metaphors played out, just as in a dream, demonstrating, as a story does, precisely what I had sought to know. Hughes, too, commenting on the pond incident, said: "It was very weird, a complete dream".

I wonder if this happens more often than we realise; if we just don't notice chains of events which, if seen as a 'story', could in a significant way inform us about something relevant, just as we don't notice many dreams either, unless they are 'big' enough. (Though to me 'not noticing' is healthier, and less irritating, than interpreting nearly everything that happens as 'meaningful' or – ghastly word in my opinion – 'meant'.)

Certainly, wherever we put our attention at any moment becomes the given reality for that moment. The anthropologist Edward T. Hall, for instance, described an incident in his childhood "when we were on a boat crossing a stormy English Channel and I was turning green." His mother quickly read him the story of *Momotaro*, the Japanese Peach Boy, and her strategy worked. The young Hall was transported to a place where seasickness was not even a possibility, and so the impending attack of it was staved off.

Focus and the locus of attention generate our sense of reality. Whether this is inward or outward seems of no consequence to the brain. I imagine this will not really come as a surprise to any readers of this journal – but even though the information is known to psychotherapists and readily available from self-observation, it is not yet part of more formal general knowledge, nor of the cultural consensus.

I remember the poet Robert Graves sometimes playing a "coincidence game", which would begin by setting the focus. He would start it over dinner, say, simply by announcing it, and from that moment on those present continue chatting as before. Nothing was expected or looked for. The one time I was present coincidences poured in. Surprising links between individuals were revealed, a chance phone call that came in during dinner almost magically tied up loose ends connecting two of the people present, and one guest's anecdote of a stranger who had helped him when a car knocked him down in Rio, and then just disappeared, turned out to be actually sitting next to him, unrecognised, at the table.

Perhaps the reason we like magicians so much is because they provide the illusion that familiar rules can occasionally be held in abeyance or briefly superseded. Perhaps we love the illusion of objects or people dematerialising and showing up elsewhere, ("Beam me up, Scotty"!) because it chimes with something in us that wants, even senses, that there may be more than one way of reading events. An eminent, hard-nosed scientist I know absolutely adores magic shows. The more he watches the apparent suspension of the ordinary rules of cause and effect and can't work out why, the happier he is.

Certainly, most of us enjoy the dream-like feeling magic provides, as if another order is operating, and feel flat when we discover how the trick was done. Was that all? Just that? The mind-opening impression and wonder of 'something else' has been removed.

(As I wondered what to say in this next paragraph, I decided to play the coincidence game with myself. Half an hour later, while tidying a cupboard – like many others, I'm a habitual tidier when the writing gets stuck – I found a book by Joseph Campbell lodged underneath piles of bedclothes, towels and old linen. It must have been there for years. Opening it at random the first words I saw were: " ... the creative interplay ... alerts the artist to the possibility of a revelatory composition in which outer and inner realities are recognised as the same."

"That'll do", I thought. "Thanks for the nudge".)

Could it be, then, that when dreams can play out in waking life, or when coincidences appear, inside and out are being brought into focus together, like a camera merging two images, both of which have similarities but are not the same? I certainly know of instances, many instances in fact, when writers seem to straddle both realities. I collect stories of such moments, when what writers spin from within themselves and set down on the page coincides with life 'out there'. I remember Hughes himself saying that he had written a line about a moth, I think it was, flying into a nostril – and a moment later precisely that happened to him. And my novelist neighbour once described a car crashing into a bus in a book he was writing, and later that morning he walked outside and saw that very accident take place.

However, if ordinary life is to remain stable, a balance must be established between inward and outward. Indeed part of the job in the therapy room can be to restore that balance. I have seen in my clients how often either the outside world or the inner dominates inappropriately, or else the one inter-penetrates the other – for example, when memories and structures from inner experience affect outward behaviour, irrespective of context.

But there are always those moments of creativity, or emergency, or sheer love, or something else, when everything just 'comes together', and whether your focus is within or outside, the picture is the same.

38

Research is not always enough

ONE OF THE fringe benefits of doing psychotherapy is that clients prompt wider questions. For example one young man was so wedded to his intellectual idea of love that over and over again he was under the impression that he had fallen deeply in love, and then felt excruciating anguish when, predictably, his script failed to tally with reality, and the object of his affections (very sensibly) walked out. It took him by surprise every single time.

This set me wondering whether society and culture sometimes work in similar ways. After all, we generally believe what the 'head' tells us, often in the teeth of the evidence, and exist within the bubble of that belief, unaware of the effect our misunderstanding has on us. The 'head' may be an authority figure, an idea, social pressure, esteemed information, or anything else which distorts our attempts to understand ourselves and our environment – including what we think we know about our enemies.

As a culture we have specialised in one excellent way of acquiring information to help us in all this. We do research. It serves us well and has taken us far. But trouble starts when (as with my client) pre-existing 'scripts' obscure objectivity. Perhaps the need for funding is stronger than the thirst for knowledge. Perhaps the methodology was suspect. Perhaps the research was undertaken to sell something. Newspapers like the scientific aura of a survey, so advertisers will often specially commission a small survey to show that, say, people who use their new product get luckier, or taller or smarter or stronger or prettier, or anything else considered newsworthy.

Some people need the backing of authority before accepting anything. Many years ago I wrote a book on human belief and included some carefully considered contentions about cult behaviour. The editor asked for my sources. "The source is my own observation over many years," I said edgily. "No good," he said. "I want an authority." "Otherwise you won't believe it?" "No, why should I?" "What if the research hasn't been done yet?" "Well, I can't just take your word." "How many people's word would you need, to accept something?" I asked. Under pressure he settled for 400. "How about 399?" I enquired nastily.

So the passage was cut from the book, to be replaced by some research results he found acceptable even though, deliberately to prove how wrong he was, I had invented both the research and the Institute it purported to emanate from. Thus I learned an important truth. My editor, and many like him, had no way of discriminating between diligent observation and spurious research – even though in this case I'd built in enough clues that the latter was a practical joke. (Some readers got the joke though, and wrote wittily to tell me so.)

My original contention was quite straightforward, by the way. Simply that cult behaviour existed everywhere in ordinary society, and that the differences between respectable institutions and extreme and dangerous cults was only one of degree. I was sure others had recognised this before me. At the time of the argument the idea must have been in the air, because a few years later it found its authority figure in psychiatrist Arthur Deikman, who wrote about cult behaviour in *The Wrong Way Home*.

I was very young when I wrote that book on belief, but that incident taught me something I've seen repeatedly since – valuable ideas may languish like orphans, while useless or questionable ones, if acceptably packaged, will be eagerly adopted.

Where once we quoted the Bible with conviction, now we quote research results. It can be illuminating, as it is when authors cram their books with research that readers like me are unaware of, and use it to provide challenging new perspectives on established ideas. However, the illumination is often short-lived. I've read dozens of books, as we all have, and been impressed by the rich vein of research the authors have mined – and then just forgotten almost all of it.

For putting research to use, of course, must wait until a need is perceived. This is a common story in the hard sciences, but in psychology, too, information can remain undigested in the gee-whizz realm until we find a chance to apply it. For example, I remember seeing hypnosis experiments where a subject became cringing and paranoid when it was suggested to her that all voices were louder than her own, and then turned into a bully when it was suggested that all voices were softer. So, when a bully picked on me at work, I simply spoke louder than he did. Within 20 minutes the wind had gone right out of his sails. And for me, information had become knowledge and experience.

But there is also so much dross!

Inane research that wastes time and money to demonstrate the obvious. Here are examples of twaddle published in recent months: a study at Leiden University investigated what influences how much regret we feel, and concluded that "uncertainty about what could have been reduces feelings of regret"; another from the same university concluded that students' racial prejudices were reduced when they shared university accommodation with roommates from a different ethnic group; and a study at Sheffield Hallam University found that people's tendencies to experience fantasies of revenge "may inhibit the likelihood of forgiving".

Even setting aside the fact that research is frequently flawed and always provisional, do we really think we know more about ourselves than people in other cultures at other times, simply because they lacked our tools and methodology? What about observation, deduction, induction, contemplation, thought experiment? What about learning from one's own and others' experience? Or the understanding that comes from being true to oneself? What, above all, about common sense – that quality which the research quoted above so conspicuously lacked?

While teaching a workshop on ethical behaviour in psychotherapy some years back I suggested that perhaps the unspoken commandment, "Thou shalt not be found out or struck off" lay behind many so-called 'ethical' decisions in our profession, and that it might be preferable to meet the needs of patients by using the more human yardsticks of good intention, consultation, and common sense. An honest therapist put up her hand. "I don't think I have any common sense," she said. "I'm not even sure I'd know what it is."

A subject for research, perhaps?

39

The pleasures within life's limits

IN THE Scottish island village where we live much of the time, a small family-run bistro offers nightly live music. One evening last summer, singer-songwriter Christine Bovill, from Glasgow, filled our minds and hearts with what could best be described as 'essence of song'. With her husky, passionate voice, and clearly a powerful mind behind it, she was like a traditional storyteller, letting the words and the music speak for themselves. Her huge talent was lightly worn and generously given – she must have worked hard over the years to come to that apparent ease. I imagine she is on the edge of a big career.

Next morning I found I couldn't follow my normal practice of listening to the BBC's *Today* programme. The honesty and humanity of the night before was still with me, and accomplished as it is in presenting issues of the day, the programme seemed at that moment petty and point-scoring, lost in worldly preoccupations – and I didn't want to let go of the lightness and cleanness of the previous night. Even now its impact is with me still: a small jewel of memory. When I checked with others who had been there, I found they too had felt the 'special', indeed exceptional, pleasure of what, outwardly at least, could be deemed a very modest event. It was a genuinely 'epicurean' experience, in fact.

And yes I *do* mean 'epicurean'. The Greek philosopher Epicurus, from whose thought the word derives, wrote that "both old and young alike ought to seek wisdom, the former in order that, as age comes over him, he may be young in good things ... and the latter in order that, while he is young, he may at the same time be old, because he has no fear of things which are to come."

He also called 'pleasure' the 'greatest good' – saying that the way to attain it was to live modestly, gain knowledge of the workings of the world, and know the limits both of life and one's desires.

I decided, out of interest, to see if – and how much – our society matched up to his ideas. And right away it became clear that one of what he calls the 'workings of the world' results in society distorting past thinkers' ideas, and reflecting instead the cultural assumptions of the day. So an epicurean is defined by my dictionary as "a person with refined taste, especially in food and wine" and/or "devoted to sensuous pleasure and luxurious living". In fact just what many of us today, egged on by the media and the advertising industry, aspire to as 'the good life'.

But our interpretation of the good life, and epicurean 'pleasure', could hardly now be described either as 'modest', or a 'search for wisdom'. Instead our minds absorb poisonous material day after day, hearing the news, scanning the Web, taking in – trance-like – whatever the media tell us about worldwide disasters, violence and thuggery. Simultaneously, we are also fed on their opposites: such as the excitements of trends and fashion, and the lemming-rush to be visible on social media or acquire the latest desirable gadget. We can't avoid it: the cyber-media 'life' hangs like a pall over us, filling us up with bite-size trivia, draining away any sense of the truth and the 'limits of things'.

Nor are we looking at our death, which is what Epicurus meant when he spoke about not fearing 'things to come'. We certainly pay attention to *news* of death – but just as long as it doesn't come too close. Way back in 1969, over a catastrophic six weeks, I lost my mother, my father, my dearest cousin, and my aunt, the cousin's mother. When I told a friend what had happened, the words escaped her before she could stop them: "Oh well, the less said about that the better," she muttered. An instance worth a thousand.

However, all of us live our daily lives in a matrix of tragedy, loss, pain and death. This is what makes each day so precious. If we do not carry the understanding within us that our time here is limited, we will inevitably dwell in the shallows, unable to properly appreciate and value our time and experience. Yet most of us behave as if we were immortal, skating over the surfaces, convinced that ... well, if life seems endless, then surely the best is yet to come.

Is this why many of those who can afford it are always on the look-out for more, better, or *best* – addicts needing stronger 'hits'? Or why we increasingly, and ludicrously, assign value to things these days by rating them – the 20 best films of all time, the 10 best books, or writers, or historical figures, or travel destinations, etc? Why the more famous someone is, the correspondingly more the interest and 'pleasure' in meeting them? Most of the time it seems to me that our consumer society is turning us into predictable 'products' rather than human beings. Indeed sometimes I wonder what's out there waiting to consume *us*. Are we also perhaps 'battery chickens' for some cosmic cannibal?

Epicurus believed that death brought total annihilation, so that if it caused no pain after we were gone, it would be foolish to allow it to do so while we lived. But whatever our belief about death, be it annihilation or a world to come, I think there is good reason to welcome it when it arrives, because ... just imagine the horror of living forever! A traditional story relates that Alexander the Great, discovering the Water of Eternal Life, is warned of the terrible fate awaiting those who drink it – and in the nick of time he abstains. And throughout the centuries, all over the world, legends which originated long before Christianity tell of a man cursed with the ultimate punishment – being condemned to walk the earth forever. Known variously as The Deathless One, the Wandering Jew, Ahaseurus, Cain, Malchus, Michob Ader, and many more, he has lived through thousands of generations and seen the rise and fall of countless cultures. But while able to help others, he cannot help himself. His story spurs us on to make the best of what we've got.

All of which brings me back to that modest evening in the Scottish bistro, remembering the harmony in the room, as 35 (or so) of us sipped our drinks and listened to Christine Bovill singing, well aware that we were sharing a pleasure beyond price. And what did she sing about? Love, longing, sorrow and loss. Life's depths and life's limits, in fact. I think it would have given Epicurus great pleasure.

40

Labelling the difficulty

THERE IS A small shop near where I live whose owner, a unique and remarkable woman, is now a friend. She designs and makes by hand stunning and very wearable clothes and sells them absurdly cheaply – because her turnover is high and she is not greedy. Regular customers include women who couldn't afford to buy such garments anywhere else, women who love beautiful clothes and fabrics, and several top models.

Many others, though, pass the unfashionably cluttered shop window without a second glance, preferring reassuringly conventional boutiques – unaware that these same shops sometimes buy armfuls of clothes from my friend and hang them on their own rails for up to five or six times the price. They may even sew on their own labels.

If you feel a metaphor coming on, you're right. The historian Daniel Boorstin once defined a celebrity as one whose name is worth more than their services, by which measure 'The Label' itself must be the most dazzling celebrity in our culture. Where once it was modestly hidden, leaving a product to speak for itself, now it is visibly flaunted, assumed to speak for the product. Indeed some labels are so desirable that a whole industry of fakes exists to mass-produce clothing and other items – all parading counterfeit labels.

In *The Image: A Guide to Pseudo-Events in America*, Boorstin claimed (back in 1961!) that illusions and fabrications had become an increasingly dominant force in society. Public life, he said, was filled with staged and scripted events that were counterfeit versions of actual happenings. And there were counterfeit people too, their identities similarly concocted to present illusions that had little or no relationship to anything real.

Most people, however, don't need PR firms for this – they can do the job themselves. The Jimmy Savile story is a warning of what can happen in an extreme case. His labels included 'devout Catholic', 'do-gooder', 'fundraiser' and, so help us, 'a lover of children' (who therefore, axiomatically, it was assumed, would never harm them). But such (or any other) labels will always 'get us' if we can't tolerate ambiguity, or hold several things in our minds at once. We may be aware of conflicting 'characters' in our own minds, for example, but we tend to ignore the fact that others have those same divisions too. Had we remembered this in Savile's case, given how many thought him 'creepy', reports of abuse might have been taken more seriously.

Alfred Korzybski memorably pointed out that the map is not the territory. But labels aren't even maps. Nor are they reliably stable. The term itself once just meant 'a piece of torn cloth'. 'Victim' only assumed its current meaning a little over 200 years ago. It was associated before that with holiness and sacrifice. Someone sleeping in a ditch is labelled 'vagrant', which once simply meant 'wanderer'. But lift the 'vagrant' label off that sleeping individual and you begin to see a multitude of possible stories.

In fact, useful as labels are, (we couldn't do much without them), we really must prise them off from time to time and see the reality underneath. Otherwise we remain unaware how upside down the world is – a state of affairs brilliantly encapsulated in a joke I got from Boorstin. Admiring Friend: "My, that's a beautiful baby you have there." The Mother: "Oh, that's nothing – you should see his photograph!"

However there is something else, seemingly very far from all this but perhaps closer than we think. There are rumours, always have been, that there are other ways of seeing. Western societies usually consider this a fantasy, probably because our cultures prize 'rationalism' and tend to ignore or render invisible anything that can't be proved by current yardsticks.

It's a long stretch, but a valid one I think, to speculate whether lifting labels off something from time to time might be a helpful step towards sometimes switching into this different way of 'seeing'. This is not a new thought (what is?) but it occurs to me because a book by Malidoma Patrice Somé has just been returned to me and fell open at the relevant page.

Patrice, originally from a small tribe in Burkino Faso, was kidnapped by the French and educated in a Jesuit seminary. Only after several years did he find his way back home. The pain and indoctrination had greatly changed him, and the tribal elders reluctantly decided that only initiation, though he was beyond the usual age, might restore him to himself – and to them.

Patrice's first initiatory task was to select a sizeable tree, sit, stand or kneel about 20 metres away, and look hard at it. There followed many hours of boredom and torment in the fierce heat, as he wondered what he was supposed to see, and what was preventing him from seeing it. He even pretended to see an antelope, to get himself off the hook. The astonished elders immediately saw through that.

Returned to the task next day, he overheard the elders saying that the reason he couldn't 'see' was because he was fighting himself – perhaps he had lived too long among white men, and (given that antelope) he had become a liar as well. However, after many more painful hours his resistance simply wears out. He resigns himself to his own emptiness, finds his simplicity and sincerity, and from within himself enters the reality within the tree. The experience is overwhelming, its form and content inconceivable until experienced, and unsayable in precise words thereafter. It was what the elders had been hoping for.

And this kind of 'seeing' is represented in Western culture too – despite the prevailing climate of rationality and scepticism. It has been described with simple clarity, for instance, in a short poem by Rilke, *What birds hurl themselves through*, written in 1924. Here, translated by David Pendlebury, is the second of the two simple stanzas:

> "Space reaches out from us, translating things:
> if you would truly grasp the being of a tree,
> cast inner space about it, from that space
> that bides within you. Wrap it in restraint.
> It knows no limits. Only when configured
> in your resignation is it truly tree."

At a time when technology and gadgets are patterning our minds, and brands and labels rule, it seems to me that whether on women's clothing, or on an assumed do-gooder, or on phenomena in the natural world, or on anything else, we don't know the half of it until the labels come off.

41

Could be worse?

IN HIS epigram *the medium is the message*, Marshall McLuhan defined a phenomenon earlier variously identified by Plato, Pope and Joyce. Later, cultural critic Neil Postman, and others, carried the discussion on 'from McLuhan's generation, arguing that new technology could never substitute for human values. From the 1960s onward I followed it all, or as much as I could understand. And in 1982 I bought my first computer.

I thought I was primed and suitably forewarned about the coming impact on my work and lifestyle. After all, in 1969, barely able to believe my eyes, I had watched a word-processing computer at work at Stanford Research Institute, and for more than a decade thereafter had been eavesdropping, fascinated, on developments in information technology. So I was well aware that (in the flatness of techie-speak) the effects would certainly be 'non-trivial'. But like most of us I seriously underestimated the extent of the upheaval and changes ahead, both personally and for society.

A couple of years after I bought the computer, I heard a radio interview which I never forgot. Dr. Robin Fawcett, linguistics researcher at the Polytechnic of Wales, was worried that "...the model that most people use to communicate with computers is too restricted. If they continue to employ it this could have serious and far-reaching consequences for the mental and social life of humanity."

The human-machine communication, he said, was in its current mode 'impoverished' in certain important ways. For instance, computers can't carry the emotional meaning implicit in most human-to-human interactions. And they can't carry on a realistic conversation for long either, because more than a tweet-sized complex sentence lies beyond their grasp.

Fawcett said: "If the language we use for talking to computers is impoverished, if the language we use for talking to each other is thereby impoverished, the language we use for thinking is going to be impoverished, and this could even put some limits on the development of future ideas by creative human thinking."

He conceded that there may ultimately be more to 'thinking' than simply 'talking to oneself', but doing just this does in fact describe the greater part of what is commonly described as 'thought'. So it should hardly be a surprise that people who spend up to 80% of their waking lives under the constraints imposed by machines will tend to carry these patterns over into much of their 'thinking' and also their face-to face interactions – particularly the young, who have no experience of a time 'Before'.

As the radio programme's presenter, Peter Evans, commented to Fawcett: "... there's a tremendous irony in what you're saying. We're trying to develop machines as it were to potentiate our own intelligence ... and we end up by undermining, depleting, going into a sort of intellectual Dark Ages."

More than 30 years on, it is clear that Fawcett's premonitions have come to pass. Though in fairness to him, he said plainly: "I'm not predicting that this is what is going to happen; I'm saying these are dangers that we ought to alert ourselves to." He had no inkling, however, of how substantially the unpleasant and dishonourable aspects of human thought and behaviour would ooze their way into the electronic media.

The various 'impoverishments' Fawcett noted have fed back into conventional human communication at all levels. For example, we have been trained to accept substandard language, with all the degradation in communication that this implies. Few organisations in recent years, for instance, have invested more money in IT than the NHS. Yet last time I visited my GP, the touch-sensitive log-in screen on the reception desk told me: "There are 1 persons ahead of you in the queue." It would be a mistake, in my opinion, to think this a trivial illustration.

There is rarely just one reason for any phenomenon, but I think that the acceptance of such substandard expression, as well as wall-to-wall commercialisation, shortening of attention span, dumbing down, loss of privacy, willingness to become subsumed into an anonymous network of others, and the absence of empathic feeling for friends – all with their attendant social consequences – are all in some large part the playing out of what McLuhan, Fawcett, and others, foresaw.

Indeed it seems paradoxical that as our means of digital 'communication' proliferate, we are, in general, less and less in true human contact with each other. At least once a week I, as you probably do too, get caught up in a computerised telephone system and realise, oh my God, I'm trapped without a map in someone else's flowchart! Then, again like you no doubt, I have to resort to native deviousness to break free. For instance, I talk gibberish at automated voices, giving them nothing they are programmed to understand, until the system yields me up to a human being.

And the effects go well beyond that. Great numbers of people now think they are communicating when in fact they are more isolated, typing or mouthing empty words which relate only to the surfaces of life. In spite of their numbers of 'friends', many individuals seem barely tuned in to the reality of anyone else. They live virtually alone in the desert of their private universe. An old joke, which is also deeply serious, sums it up wonderfully:

Two old acquaintances meet after not having seen each other for some years. "How are you?' the first asks. "Terrible" comes the reply. "Why's that?" "You remember my business, how well it was doing?" "Yes". "Well it went bust. I lost everything."

"Sorry to hear that," says the first man. "But it could have been worse."

"You haven't heard the whole story. You remember my wife Miriam?" "Yes. Beautiful girl." 'Well, not long after the business collapsed, she suddenly died."

"Oh dear! But it could have been worse."

"Wait. There's more. I married again, and my new wife ran off with my remaining money."

"Poor you. But still, it could have been worse."

"Could have been worse!" screamed the unfortunate fellow.

"Haven't you heard anything I've said? How could it have been worse?"

Said the other: "Well, it could have happened to me."

42

Up and down
the stream

EVERY SO OFTEN someone hands you a metaphor so memorable and penetrating that it becomes a yardstick, part of your vocabulary. One such runs right through *Taking Appearance Seriously* by Henri Bortoft, a physicist, teacher, philosopher and historian of science. It lights up the perpetual confusion between an experience at the moment it's happening and facets of that experience which can be thought about after the event. Moreover, it helps one see the muddle and misconceptions that can flow from it, and where the remedy lies.

The metaphor came about because Bortoft was due to teach a series of workshops on phenomenology – and, being young and enthusiastic at the time, had agreed to do so without having any clear idea how to go about it. As the deadline loomed, he was still floundering, and growing increasingly anxious. The day before, he went for a country walk to calm himself, and arrived in a valley through which ran a small, clear river.

"I stood on a bridge", he says, "looking downstream at the river flowing away from me. For some reason this made me feel uneasy, and I crossed to the other side to look at the river flowing towards me. This felt better, and I spent some time there, looking upstream. I began to be drawn into the experience of looking, plunging with my eyes into the water flowing towards me. When I closed my eyes I sensed the river streaming through me, and when I opened them again, I found that I was experiencing the river flowing towards me outwardly and through me inwardly at the same time. The more I did this, the more relaxed and free from anxiety I began to feel.

"But of course, the moment eventually came for the first workshop to begin. I remember walking ... toward the room where it was to take place, feeling I was about to be extinguished ... Instead, as I walked into the room, I heard myself saying, with surprising confidence: 'Our problem is that where we begin is already downstream, and in our attempt to understand where we are we only go further downstream. What we have to do instead is learn how to go back upstream and flow down to where we are already, so that we can recognise this as not the beginning but the end. That's phenomenology!' I don't know who was more surprised, myself or the students."

So while many ingredients comprise an experience, the experience itself remains One and indivisible. There is always a distance between the living experience, upstream, and the brain's subsequent downstream 'model' or 're-presentation' of it, in which elements of that experience are not intrinsically bound-as-one, but can be named, considered, manoeuvred, or even deliberately ignored. Like leaves in the river, they can float ever further downstream, ever more disconnected from the reality which inspired them.

Cartoonists, those masters of metaphor, have often showed up the division between an actual, upstream phenomenon and what we find further down. One *New Yorker* cartoon, for example, has a dumpy wife watching as her portly husband points at items on a flipchart. He has listed and ticked off various elements in their life, such as 'solvent', 'fully insured', 'kids OK', 'we have our health' and 'we have each other', and drawn a neat line under the list – and underneath that, his conclusion: Total = Happiness. His wife looks dubious. Clearly all these parts don't add up to her experience of their married state. Indeed the caption has her saying: "Could you run that by me one more time please Walter".

Another cartoon I've enjoyed offers a version for our times of Aesop's tale of *The lion and the mouse*. The mouse has evolved into a doctor in a white coat, stethoscope round his neck, towards whom the lion, his patient, is holding out a paw, a thorn clearly stuck in it. Mouse-doctor is looking but not touching. The caption has the mouse saying: "Yes it *is* thornlike in appearance, but I think I need to order a battery of tests." Easy to see that the mouse-doctor has taken up residence downstream, and is about to spend unnecessary time and money. And easy to see, too, in the earlier example, that the husband believes that by adding up those aspects of the marriage he thinks count, he has actually represented the upstream experience.

I have glimpsed profound depths in Bortoft's metaphor, but meaning pours from it even where I am, in the shallows, and others will find meanings of their own. I have seen, for instance, that politicians manipulate whatever pieces of the downstream model suit their purpose. For example, compassion, downstream, becomes a commodity which can be squeezed out of nursing – whereas compassion, upstream, belongs inherently within the phenomenon of nursing, and is utterly indivisible from it. Psychotherapists sometimes encounter in their clients all manner of unhappiness and disturbance proliferating from a single difficult experience further up. Even pressure of time when writing e-mails may send us further downstream, to say what we didn't really mean.

These days we seem to be in increasing thrall to downstream thinking, trying to make sense of things by going even further downstream, instead of going back up to find the living connection. I remember how, as a white child in apartheid South Africa, I would hear the cruel dogma, relentlessly repeated, that all non-white people were 'inferior'. But any child could see that skin colour was only skin deep, and that the unique, undifferentiated human reality was elsewhere – upstream, I could now say.

Even so, there were always some visitors to our country behaving differently. I remember, for instance, watching an Englishman talking to a black garage attendant. Simply by his demeanour he demonstrated to anyone with eyes to see that he must have come from a place – I mean a mentality, not a geographical location – where skin colour wasn't particularly an issue. It wasn't what visitors like him said. It was how, innately, they were. By simply being themselves, they gave us hope.

The black friends with whom, against the odds, I managed to talk saw it too. And the visitors exemplified something else beyond our experience as well – that they must have come from a country, indeed that there must actually *be* such a country, where colour discrimination was not enshrined in law. For me, young and unknowing, that instant flash of wonder, understanding and energy was an unforgettable upstream experience.

Bortoft's metaphor also throws light on the world's enduring stories – how by 'living' them upstream, within our imaginations, they prepare us to see and understand their pattern, should we meet an element of that pattern in downstream life. Indeed, it seems to me that to live and evolve in this world, human beings need to be able to switch their attention up and down the flowing stream – and now and then, as Bortoft did on the bridge, actually plunge into the flow.

Sadly, Henri died just a few months before writing these words, shortly after *Taking Appearance Seriously* was published. His book is challenging but immensely rewarding, far more so than my rudimentary account of his central metaphor would indicate – but one has to put in the work. I like to imagine that death took Henri as far upstream as any human being can go.

43

Making the invisible visible

IN THE early 1960s I wrote a handful of television documentaries. My first script took all the time it needed, came out just as I conceived it, and actually won an award. My last, called *The Way We Live Now*, was rather less rewarding.

At the initial conference the producer asked me for script ideas. "Well let's get what we don't want out of the way", I said. "I banged out an outline script last night, just by stringing together the usual clichés and formulae." The director read it. "But this is exactly what we want!", he said. "No!" I blurted. "You can't mean that?" "Look Pat," he said patiently. "The budget allows three weeks for each programme. We haven't time to reinvent the wheel. You've done it. We'll make it!"

This shift from pleasure to disappointment in my work exactly mirrored a revolution in television culture. In the space of a year, power had moved from the creative teams to the accountants. Where I, a freelancer, had still looked for fruitful discussion, the producer, an employee, was now serving the new constraints, oblivious, it seemed, to how we had once worked.

The same thing was happening in many organisations. Vital, if invisible, concepts, values and possibilities – the unthinkable thought, the potential quality, the germ of a realisation – were being rendered down, as accounting, money, and measurement took over. Later, 'mission statements' were brought in. They *had* to be, to represent now, in a few words, the substance of what had been lost – the unspoken understanding of the 'mission' itself.

Thereafter came the rush to targets, league tables, tick-boxes and profits. Of course there is seldom any point in making a loss, but neither need the one and only goal be the largest possible financial profit.

And so here we are. The Way we Live Now. For many people, modesty has been replaced by 'bigging yourself up'; charity, best done in the dark, has become a matter of display; respect and esteem are seen as entitlement; generosity towards others is overshadowed by acquisition for self; and love is sought as if it were a commodity. So much forgotten, so fast.

We've all seen it. When budgets at schools needed cutting, 'story time' was often the first victim. No matter that our priceless heritage of stories are vital for growing minds. They are useless to league tables.

Similarly compassion, at the very heart of nursing, at the time of writing lies comatose under the weight of concrete targets and academic milestones. Students no longer learn from experienced nurses at the bedside of patients – by osmosis, so to speak. But how else can you learn to nurture sick individuals, and tune in to what they need, without 'catching it' from one who understands?

Again, libraries close, because Councils look at outward facts – 42 per cent of adults visited a library only twice in the last two years, paperbacks are cheap, and the Web supplies more content, more quickly, than library reference sections.

But the research doesn't look at the years of degrading library conditions and book stocks. And it certainly can't measure the humanity within libraries – the atmosphere of calm and thought, the happy intervention of the 'library angel' guiding a browser's hand, the opportunity for old codgers to come out of the cold and pore over newspapers, for mothers to meet at playgroups, for the exchange of community skills and interests via the physical locus of the notice-board, for the life of a child to be transformed by entering an Aladdin's cave of books.

Well-meaning people have suggested remedies to restore what's been lost, but they usually talk in terms of 'management' and 'leadership', as if they themselves were mere spectators waiting to be managed or led – while the spirit within the heart of stories, or nursing, or libraries, for the most part languishes unseen, unfed, uninvoked.

Indeed how can we find words, let alone legislate, for the intangibles that have fled? The terms in which I speak of them here are laughably vague: 'touch', 'feel', 'taste', 'tuning in', even 'sniffing' these things, or 'catching' their scent. How much easier, these days, to look straight through and past this sensory spectrum – hinting as it does at consciousness, authenticity, and inner significance – as if it didn't exist.

In *Life, The Universe, and Everything*, Douglas Adams describes how "the technology involved in making something properly invisible is so mind-bogglingly complex that ... it's simpler just to ... do without it. The 'Somebody Else's Problem field'", he says, "is much simpler, more effective, and can be run for over a hundred years on a single torch battery", because "it relies on people's natural predisposition not to see anything they don't want to, weren't expecting, or can't explain."

Tellingly, given the spirit of our times, the technology of invisibility has recently made great strides. We actually can reflect light back from, or round, an object now, and so look straight through it. YouTube has film clips which demonstrate this. But as all good therapists and teachers know, to make visible something disregarded but of real value, we actually need to throw light *on* it, and *look*.

Thus by a mental switch I can see that all over our country, people as decent as they can manage to be in such difficult times, go about their business, doing the best they can, grateful for what they have, learning whenever possible, and mystified by the ludicrous self-centred lives so many of us live, myself included. Dazzled as we are by media glitz and our sense of entitlement, these honourable people are usually invisible to us. But without their existence, I think our lives would be far worse.

And suddenly I remember, as a child, hearing the adults talking in shocked tones about a man they once knew who had fallen into poverty. He was living in a rundown shack at the time, but had on his wall a valuable painting which had belonged to his great-grandfather: in the foreground, an old man, face and posture suffused with humanity, experience and acceptance, and behind him, a gently blazing landscape. Galleries and dealers had offered the pauper vast sums for it, relatives had thundered at him to sell it and live decently, but he stubbornly ignored them all. To him that painting represented precious qualities that shone through and beyond canvas and frame, and nothing would get him to part with it.

Seen in that light, though we seem to have lost so much, perhaps 'the way we live now' isn't so different from the way we lived then.

44

What it is that
really counts

AS I STARTED typing this sentence, the world population was 7,358-341,401. Less than seven seconds later, when I finished, 41 individual presences had arrived on our planet, and 16 others had left.

If you want to watch the relentless to and fro of human traffic, go to www.worldometers.info/world-population The numbers whizz past at dizzying speed. Given the likelihood that not all births and deaths are reliably recorded everywhere, world population may be even more than the 7.3 billions I saw. Indeed some millions more may have arrived by the time you read this.

So numbers rise, people come and go, turning up at roughly three times the rate of those who leave. But what is even more mind-boggling than the colossal numbers, as billions crowd into the planet ever faster, is that *no two of us are exactly the same*. We are physiologically different from birth. No two fingerprints are the same. Even identical twins are different, and more so as the years go by.

And we are especially different where it matters most – in the essential part of ourselves which is *us;* that sense of ourselves which has always felt the same, and which no one can take away from us. As I've mentioned before, it is an understanding instantly communicated in the memorable words of a five-year-old girl, who on hearing that one of our family friends was pregnant, asked with intense interest: "Who is she getting for a baby?"

Every person I have ever met has had a special 'flavour' which suffuses everything about them – an unsayable 'taste' which marks them out as individual and distinct. Even though indoctrination and conditioning can draw a veil over our true selves, sometimes for almost a lifetime, the potential of 'who' we are is above and beyond such distortions.

But if we *are* all such unique individuals, then where *is* everybody? This thought has been prompted, time and again, by clients who seem utterly, almost wilfully, unaware of their core self, and have done their best to become someone else – usually some idealised creature engineered by social, economic and media pressures.

The most recent client like this, a woman in her early 40s, grew up in a comfortable home, but was given warmth and attention only when she was deemed 'good', by which her religious parents meant 'self-denying'. Throughout her adult life she worked hard to tick all the right boxes, and become likeable, charming, interesting, and a high achiever. She also compulsively sought partners, one after another, good men all, to supply the confidence she lacked. But as soon as they wobbled, showing their own vulnerability – usually some time after the 'honeymoon' period – her feeling for them abruptly switched off. She would reject them coldly, without negotiation, and move on to the next man.

She was, in fact, a construct built over a chasm – quite unaware that, vulnerable or not, she was valid and valuable in her own right. She may have been counted by the world population clock, but she had never counted herself. Like so many others, she had been wandering in a wilderness, unaware of how close she actually was to what she sought.

The sciences, brilliant as they are in their own domain, are not much help in the search for self. I once read, for example, a brief scientific description of the design and function of a human head which, by deliberately refraining from spelling out that this was the topic under consideration, demonstrated (to me at least) how disconnected outward description can be from reality; how infinitely more exists for the individual actually inhabiting the head. But then language in itself is only one thread. The 'more' is transmitted and received only when individuals are in sufficient harmony with each other to 'get' it.

In fact when a group of people can work harmoniously together towards a common aim, without 'roles' or theories or personal agendas getting in the way, a noticeable something 'extra' is produced. I'm sure many people have had experiences of this. One of my own occurred during the apartheid era in South Africa, when I co-wrote a musical which exploded on the scene and became a landmark in South African theatrical and social history. It broke records, changed the lives of everyone connected with it, propelled a handful of our performers to lasting international fame, and has never been forgotten. Almost six decades later, recordings of the production are still on sale.

When I reflect on what made the event so exceptional, I see that not only was the time right, but that we were all so *different* – almost 90 people with different ethnicities and skin shades, different beliefs, and different backgrounds – from poverty and oppression to comfort and privilege. But all of us left our obstacles and prejudices and external differences at the door, so to speak, and worked harmoniously together, simply as ourselves, even at times against the law. We brought our effort and talent, and whatever else was necessary, while asking (for the most part) very little in return. It was because of this mental posture, I am convinced, and the fact that our essential differences were such an asset, that the show gave back a thousandfold.

I think that such extraordinary events demonstrate what can happen when we express unimpeded the humanity deep within us – the reality of which, paradoxically, is absent when too many like-minded people are collected together. You don't get harmony when everybody sings the same note. And you don't get humanity unless the note is true and the voice sincere.

There are so many people now. Many may be little more than 'constructs', as my former client was. Many more, myself included, have been fashioned and manipulated for the most part by our generation and society – yet not completely, or all the time, thank goodness. And it is in this other part of ourselves that there exists, indestructible I think, the deep drive of humanity to express itself through us. If there were more of us who felt that just being ourselves was sufficient, or the best or the only place to start, as happily my former client now does, might it just be that humanity would stand a better chance of surviving these perilous times?

It is noon some days later as I type these final words. So far 200,445 more people have arrived today, each one bringing with them something unique. But even though 7.3 billion humans is a stupendous number – especially for those of us who remember when it was 1.5 billion – in the arithmetic of consciousness, whose principal terms are 'One' and 'All', it fades into insignificance.

45

The sad paradox
of the kidult

CHILDREN, on the whole, can't wait to grow up. They anticipate and rehearse, imitate parents and older siblings, stretch themselves towards the future. These days, however, it seems there's actually a trend in the other direction. Research shows that more and more people in their twenties and even thirties are living with their parents, thus in many ways and habits, extending their childhood circumstances.

The commercial marketplace even has a name for them. It categorises them as 'kidults, adultescents, rejuveniles or twixters', names as awkward as the condition. According to the Entertainment Software Association, for instance, the average age of video game players is now 31, up from 18 in 1990. Disney World is the No. 1 *adult* vacation destination in the world, visited by huge numbers without a child in tow. And all around us we see the 'toyification' of everyday items from cars to computers (lilac-coloured iMacs) to kitchen gadgets (with clown and animal faces).

The more immature and dissatisfied these adult children are, the more they will delightedly buy such things on impulse. But their unrealistic expectations of life makes them therapist-fodder too, because almost inevitably depression awaits them. The kidult's unvoiced cry, expressed through a thousand different demands, is "if I can't get what I want the world will end". Life may be rather like the weather, coming and going regardless of our wishes, but kidults insist that every day should be perfect.

For instance one of my clients wanted to find and 'install' a husband before her (perfectly healthy) father died, because she feared she couldn't manage without someone to do the jobs around the house. Sometimes women on their own want to have a child, "so someone will love me", as this seems easier than achieving an adult relationship. Then there are the men of all ages, hard and tough certainly – but omnipotent as babies. And others still entangled with their mothers, selfish and demanding as infants, first manipulating a mothering response from girlfriends or wives – then blaming them for behaving like their mothers do.

I once heard clinical psychologist Michael Yapko, when talking to a depressed, over-dependent patient, use the example of a mother-bear's behaviour. He described how she protects her cubs fiercely, teaching them to hunt, forage, fish, and survive in the forest, and how when they are about two years old she chases them up a tree – and abandons them. The whimpering cubs search desperately for her, until eventually it dawns on them that they are on their own and must fend for themselves. The mother has activated survival patterns within them, and her job is done.

So do we Westerners need an effective way to move our children forward, as earlier societies did, as tribal societies still do, as even a bear does? Several years ago, friends of mine who live in a small village thought so, and enacted an old Celtic ritual through which eight-year-old boys were given into the care of their fathers. The mother told me: "The three of us went to a bridge across a stream. My husband went to the far side. Then I gave my son a big hug, mentally cut a golden cord I visualised between us, and he walked across the bridge on his own, towards his dad. On the other side his father embraced him, and they took off on a walk together."

Very sensibly, my Celtic friends kept this metaphorical acting-out light, personal, and informal. In the Arab world also, I am told, boys of about eight are, equally informally, expected to spend most of their time with the men. And indeed, within living memory in our own society, before all the huge changes, there were experiences that created rites of passage – war and national service for men, the responsibilities of looking after siblings, and then a family, for women.

However the rite of passage, the initiation, was never more than what the word implies – the introduction, at a deep level, of a concept which initiates would begin to manifest in themselves, and over time consciously strengthen and make their own. I think it was probably crucial in societies which were very cohesive, and where information from the traditions and sciences, including psychology, was not as available as it is to us today.

On the whole, however, mythopoeic rituals concocted in modern men's and women's groups in an attempt to move people forward, tend to be culty, artificial or empty. Those few 'initiates' I've met seemed too full of the wonder of it, too self-absorbed and unconvincing, too eager to spread the word.

But now comes the paradox. Far from cutting childhood short, we actually *need* it extended. Learning to live well takes time, and has to be nurtured, and we are specialised for this. Humans retain juvenile characteristics considerably longer than their closest relatives in the animal kingdom (the biological process is known as neoteny), and this creates enormous advantages in evolutionary terms, because it allows time to educate, train and develop young people's potential before sexual maturity sets in. Indeed, many cultures, ours among them, have bolted on even more time by further holding back the onset of sexual activity by means of taboos and restrictions.

Adolescents, of course, live in a haze of sex. It goes with the territory, but until recently what they thought and did about it was censored from adult awareness. Today, though, young minds are permitted, even encouraged, to focus on sexual behaviour, including what was once deemed deviant or perverted.

Even the horror of paedophilia, because it is made so public, increases this fixation. Children come to sexual maturity younger, one in three have seen pornography by the age of 10, and explicit sex in films and online has turned it into a performance sport. Consequently we see in the therapy room confused young people painfully insecure about their appearance and sexual 'accomplishment'.

Emotional, moral, and educational development, in all its necessary subtlety, is drowned out in this sea of sexual noise. Restraint, 'taking care', thought for others, discipline, the understanding needed to 'walk in another's shoes', the ability to take responsibility, self-knowledge, and the capacity to think, all of which the culturally extended childhood attempted to awaken and initiate, if not always successfully inculcate ... much of this is being traded for (notionally) bigger, better and earlier orgasms. Kidults may be childish, but they have been robbed of the innocence that would allow them to become mature while retaining a childlike purity.

46

Where do you draw the line?

ONE BALMY DAY last summer, I came upon a group of bemused people gazing at a handwritten notice stuck next to the mailing slots in the post office wall. Moments later I was as slack-jawed as they, reading with disbelief: "The ergonomic position of this pillar box is causing health and fitness issues for the staff that maintain the clearance from this collection point. This collection point will be closed until a solution/another pillar box can be installed that is fit for purpose...."

That notice, now nicely printed, is currently displayed beside a temporary postbox inside. But the mail-slots, which to my knowledge have been there about 50 years, remain sealed. Infuriatingly, we can only mail our letters in office hours.

So while the notice has been improved, the situation has not – a pattern of priorities we see whenever a line of common sense is crossed. A practice which was reasonable and helpful goes into reverse.

'Health and Safety', of course, provides countless illustrations of this pattern, simultaneously entertaining and depressing, and we all have our own stories to tell. One which to me illustrates the pattern perfectly is the closure of various Scottish 'bothies', those basic shelters in remote mountainous areas – unlocked, equipped with a few simple amenities, and available to hill walkers and climbers in sudden need. And why closed? Because they were 'unsafe' – having an entrance but no alternative exit. So somewhere along that line I mentioned, in safety's name safe refuge is denied.

But we must also remember that 'Health and Safety' legislation was introduced in the first place because of callousness, carelessness and real hazards, mainly in the work place. Given conscience and care, we wouldn't have needed the extra regulation. And nor would we be wasting time and money when well-intentioned and useful

H&S work morphs, somewhere along that line, into a callousness of its own, albeit cloaked in those three caring words.

The process is, of course, the mark of closed minds and bureaucratic thinking – rules set in stone, applied without discrimination, with no sense of, or even interest in, when the line between usefulness and obstruction has been crossed. It seems to be a primitive tendency of the human mind – to take an idea or a metaphor and make it so one-dimensional and concrete that flexibility is impossible. (Perhaps this is one explanation of the ancient warning about 'graven images'?)

However this kind of thinking goes well beyond bureaucracy or H&S silliness. Recently, for example, I was reading a book in which the author, a scientist, sneered at the ridiculous idea of being able to feed 5,000 people with five loaves and two fishes. "It's a metaphor, you goon", I wanted to screech at this usually likeable and (within his own sphere) coruscatingly brilliant man, "and I for one have experienced its reality more than once".

So there it is again, sense turned into nonsense because lines, boundaries and labels, which we create or find, very usefully, all over the place, become over-extended. This author was so constrained by his need not to seem irrational that he went too far, well over that line, missed a chance to deepen his understanding – and fell into the folly of assuming that other people were the fools.

However the essence of personal freedom is surely the capacity to discriminate – to cross lines, break rules, and take the consequences when those rules harm us or others.

We see this confusion of lines and borders in the current challenges to tyrannical regimes. We know the sad litany – Iraq, Zimbabwe, Ivory Coast, Syria, Libya… the long list of places in which brutal abusers-of-power stamp out all opposition, along with anyone else who happens to be in the way.

Within our very biology, the impulse of compassion moves us to want to help the victims. My own useless heart is typical, and aches, just as yours must do, at the ugliness and pain, the torture, the cold or frenzied murder, whether of one individual or thousands. Help them we must, if we can. It is, as we know, a human imperative.

But here again we find that stupefying line. "If you help one," someone will say, "then what about all the others?" But we need only to do what we can, as a simple tale you may know makes clear. A freak wave washes up thousands of sea-creatures onto an Australian beach, all lying there struggling and dying. Word spreads. Scores of gaping spectators arrive. A lone man is picking up the stranded creatures, one by one, and returning them to the water. A spectator sees the futility. He says: "why bother, you won't make any difference". Without breaking step the man returns another creature to the sea, saying: "Well, it made a difference to that one".

When I was young, I dreamed I was on a beach, at the water's edge, and a man was drawing lines in the sand, illustrating our familiar world to some of us. Then he said: "Actually it's not quite like that. Look." And I remember my amazement as he redrew the 'map', very simply shifting and adjusting the lines he'd first made, regrouping some elements of the picture and disconnecting others – creating different categories, different understandings, different and deeper and sometimes almost inconceivable perceptions of what had been familiar ground. It was as if he'd drawn back a curtain. Both in my dream, and after, the knowledge that such rich and astonishing reorientation was possible filled me with awe and gratitude.

So in these brave, confused and violent days, it seems to me that to be useful we need to ask ourselves, instance by instance, and so must our societies, where the lines are: What's my capacity here? What's my responsibility? What my resources? What proportion or element of this impulse is self-interest? And at any point: have I stepped over the line from sense into absurdity?

If we extend help because of what's in it for us, fair enough, but we should acknowledge the trade-off. The action may or may not be any worse for that, but we should be clear and open about where that line is. Self-interest is always present, of course it is – but if one can make it enlightened self-interest, so much the better.

And if we really don't know what to do, then all we can do is our best, and try to stay on the sane side of that line, learning as we go. In the end, that in itself might improve our health and safety.

47

I wanna see
the manager

GROWING UP in South Africa through the long years of apartheid, it was impossible not to see all around me the ugly inhumanity with which most white people behaved towards black, and my child's heart went out unreservedly to those insulted, down-trodden people.

By adolescence I had become deeply identified with them, and regarded our unhappy country far too simply, as being contaminated by the bad intentions and cruelty of the oppressors. If those people could only change their perception and behaviour, so I thought then, sanity could establish itself in the lunatic asylum we inhabited. In the meantime, I would try to live as if I was free, as if the restrictions of apartheid did not exist. And as this was a personal, not a political, commitment, I would at the same time try not to draw attention to myself.

Some further years on I realised that the roles of goody and baddy were not so clear cut: the sickness in the air infected us all. For instance I remember my shock, after (illegally) visiting a dying man of 'mixed race', at hearing him complain that he had to share a ward with 'these blacks'. And then my further shock when I finally admitted into awareness the fact that I was a racist too, in all sorts of covert and conditioned ways that I had been cunningly hiding from myself.

So I know from very early experience that if something unpleasant is in the air, we are likely to catch it one way or another, no matter what our opinions or biases may be. Here's another example. In the late 1960s I watched hippies on a Mediterranean island denouncing the consumer society, and taking great pride in rejecting its values. With a sharp eye for beauty, they had taken over *en masse* the island's loveliest beach, its sparkling sands shaded by ancient palms, and in doing so had effectively kept others from using it. Then bit by bit they had churned it up and created a slum: cramming rubbish and old food into clefts and holes in the trunks of the palms, and scattering the sands with litter. From time to time, only slightly more in sorrow than in anger, monks from a nearby monastery would come down early in the morning, while the hippies slept, and do their best to clean it up.

I would overhear these same hippies self-righteously denouncing capitalism and materialism. Yet they swarmed into the island's interior like locusts, separating the peasants from their family heritage of artefacts, swapping cheap transistor radios for needlework, rare hand-woven fabrics and wonderfully crafted objects, some of them generations old. And then they would glory at the spoils they took away, and the bargains they had managed to wangle.

On the analogy that fish aren't conscious of water until they are without any, so we on the whole are oblivious of this particular contamination in our air – the consumerism which distorts and poisons our awareness and actions. 'Retail therapy' – which unless out of control is relatively harmless – really works. We do feel great on a shopping spree, because we are doing exactly what society programmes us to do, as easily as one-two-three: See-Want-Get. So it's not surprising that we often find the same pattern in the therapy room.

All of us are affected by consumerism, of course, but the thinking of certain of my clients actually unbalanced by it goes something like this – not quite the American Declaration of Independence or Consumers' Charter, but implicitly flavoured by both: "I have the Right to feel good, just as I have the Right to a life without pain, love without blemish, money without effort, and friends without number. So if I'm not getting one or all of these things in exchange for my efforts, then something's wrong. And if something's wrong, then I must exercise my further Right – to complain and keep complaining till I get it fixed." It puts me in mind of a song, written by Alan Tunbridge in the 1960s:

> "Talkin' about a small hotel
> On a corner of the milky way
> Looking at a billion residents
> Checkin' in and checkin' out every day

Well I ain't been here long
But I can see there's somethin' wrong
And when I get through the press
at the reception desk
I'm gonna hit that bell and say:
I wanna see the manage-uh..."

You could almost call 'wanting to see the manager' a 'presenting problem' in therapy. At some unspecified point in the past, it seems, a number of guests of our small hotel placed an order, perhaps with room service, along the lines of "bring me an ideal life, a huge platter of happiness, and a side order of immunity from mistakes". And when it isn't promptly delivered, they stubbornly sit it out, session after session, in the manager's complaints department, otherwise known as the therapy room. There they cling on to fixed ideas and expectations about what they want and how therapy should proceed, waiting for the complaint to be remedied and contributing little or nothing to the proceedings.

I suppose an extreme case, the 'instance worth a thousand', in Goethe's wonderful phrase, is that of a 23-year-old client I'll call Jack. I felt enormously sorry for him. He had done virtually nothing in his whole life. Even collecting the dole was too much trouble. He sat home day after day, smoking dope and watching TV, living on handouts from his exasperated uncle. He was in therapy only because his uncle refused to support him any longer unless he came to see me weekly.

I asked Jack what he would really like to do in life, and at first that stumped him. When I persisted, he cudgelled his brains and finally conceded that he supposed it might be quite nice to run a bar in Spain. So I worked backwards from this goal with him, step by step, showing him what it would be necessary for him to do and achieve, at each point, to reach his objective.

Before we even finished he was bored. But then a secret look came over his face. There *was* a dream, he admitted. Something he had always wanted to do. In fact he thought about it for large chunks of every day. "What is it?" I asked, thinking he might at last be about to produce the key to unlock his motivation. "Winning the lottery," he said. Trying to keep a straight face, I told him: "Save your money! You've more chance of being run over by a bus." Then the old joke literally played itself out! "No, it's OK," he said. "I don't ever actually buy a ticket."

Please believe me, I am not ridiculing him – or any other individual – in what I have written here, for if I were, I would also be ridiculing myself. But I am ridiculing the expectation which infects us to the point of pathology very often – that it is possible to have it all, when one wants it, and on one's own terms.

Over the years, I have found that the 'human givens brief therapy' approach is usually quick, realistic and successful. But though I can help most of the disgruntled customers of our small hotel, sitting it out, waiting for the complaints department to deliver satisfaction, I can't help them all.

I think I can usually tell at the outset who will be the difficult ones. First, there are the 'therapy junkies', who seek a different therapist for each new psychological twinge, and know far more than I do about what is out there and on offer. They taste one therapy after another, then toss them away when the initial buzz subsides. With them, I am aware of being judged against what others say or advertise, and found wanting: a fair finding, because I really don't know how to deal with people like that.

Then there are those who are 'stuck' in therapy and who (rather like others may switch diets or astrologers or hairstyles) carry their pain very carefully, like a pet, from one therapist to another. Their requirement is that we too should stroke and groom that pet. And the bells of the complaints department ring loudly and indignantly when we offer instead to set them free from the tyranny of their little darlings.

Others won't let anything go – because they've paid for it. They are, psychologically speaking, like those hoarders who clutter their houses with papers and photographs and possessions until they are driven almost mad by them, but still can't resolve to throw them out. Extreme cases are akin to those little old ladies found living in flats blocked solid with walls of old newspaper, and only very narrow walkways in between. These people really do want to move, but are dizzied by the confusion of sheer 'stuff' in their minds. As in any ordinary house move, they must sort and throw away: but the consumerist desire to keep hold of possessions overpowers them.

Mild cases are treatable, extreme cases take longer, often, than they or I can bear.

Yet others cast their dilemmas as theatre, and invite one to admire and applaud. I remember some years back a woman possessing beauty, wealth, social standing, sufficient professional success, a loving husband, charming children and doting admirers, who saw her life as tragedy – because she also wanted recognition as a poet. She was in torment, she would say with anguish: without fame her life had no meaning. Seven years of therapy before we met had not helped. Usually I'm adept at breaking up black-and-white thinking, but not here: this woman was implacable.

Then there are those hungry for love, who drive the chance of it away by demanding it as a prerequisite. One of my current clients really accepted this idea – for a while. She seemed to understand that being thankful for what she had could make her happier and help her move forward. But then one day she said: "I've been good for six months now. How long do I have to endure this ache for love? When am I going to get my reward?"

Without exception, all these people tell me in one way or another that at times they feel they are in hell. This is the pain of extreme consumerism working in them, and the consequence of something else too: the idea of the trade-off, the contract, the bargain.

For example, if getting together with someone is a gamble, my client hungry for love has more than once invested thousands – so to speak – on a throw of the dice, not even noticing that the object of her affections has risked only a fiver. Each time, she is devastated when the investment does not work. The reason? She follows the rules of her implicit contract with life: if I pay dearly enough, the powers that be must deliver.

Those who carry their unhappiness around like pets are also prepared to pay, as long as their implicit bargain is met: if they suffer enough, and dwell on it enough, that will trigger their reward. Those who can't let anything go are constantly bargaining for more time or more space. The therapy junkies will make efforts only when their conditions are met – that the therapy must proceed in precisely the way they expect it to, and be 'delivered' in a form they have preconceived. While the woman who wants fame, though prepared to work, is grimly determined it must be on her terms.

All have made an unspoken contract with the gods or *djinns* or forces of nature, however it is they describe such things. They will pay, but there are strings. The poor boy wanting to win the lottery without buying a ticket provides an exaggerated pattern of this. But it is a template also found in people who function better than he: if we do such and such (which, note, we chose to do anyway) then we'll reap the reward.

We can see the pattern very clearly in religious terms. Many religious believers feel they have a contract with God. They will be pious and god-fearing and play by the rules, and in return they expect a successful life on earth, and a place in heaven when they die. Like consumers everywhere, they see nothing wrong in being paid twice.

But what happens when these god-fearing individuals think they are keeping their side of the bargain, only to find that things are going badly wrong? Some begin to wonder whether the other party is abiding by His side of the agreement. If this thought persists, they may bitterly conclude that God has broken the contract, leaving them free to do as they please. In other words, if God isn't delivering, they'll go to the Devil.

In secular terms, of course, there is no brimstone, no smell of sulphur, no dramatic entry of the manager of the Hotel Down There. Only a decision that the rules can now be flouted, the end will justify the means, and payment will be deferred until the order is fulfilled – a far more satisfactory arrangement than being 'good' for a period of time, and then after a long wait 'getting' nothing.

In his seminal book on the source of Freud's ideas, *Sigmund Freud and the Jewish Mystical Tradition*, which I am constantly surprised how few people have read, author David Bakan writes: "The Devil notion has associated with it a feature which we might call that of aid-in-deep-despair. The Devil is supposed to have great powers and is characteristically called upon when all else has failed. He is a terrible cure, but a powerful one nonetheless. Characteristically the Devil is approached with [in Freud's words] 'the audacity of one who has little or nothing to lose'.

The idea of selling one's soul to the devil is a powerful one. As Bakan says: "The new contract is entered into because, with the loss of hope, the anguish turns into despair; for despair is exactly anguish without hope of relief. The devil is then a cure for despair."

I haven't managed to do justice to the profundity of Bakan's remarkable work, but I quote it here because his words helped me begin at least to understand – among much else in his book – the power of this enduring metaphor. Of course the clients I have described are not – in spite of what they say – in hell. To continue the metaphor, they are not suffering the fires of the damned, but the pains of purgatory. And therein lies hope.

48

We're all
'us'

JOE WAS A butcher, physically powerful, full of laughter, bursting with life – and utterly unpolitical. In the bleak days of South Africa's apartheid, he was arrested at the funeral of his old school friend, a freedom fighter, scooped up with scores of others, and held without charge for the legal limit of 90 days, mostly in solitary confinement. Then he was freed and instantly re-arrested for another 90 days, then freed and re-arrested again. Thereafter the police dumped him on a dusty road in the middle of nowhere, and left him to make his own way back to Johannesburg.

The first night home he spent with his wife, and the second with three close friends, of whom I was one. He was skin and bone now, almost transparent. I expected him to be bitter, and possibly fiercely politicised. Instead he wanted to talk, quietly and thoughtfully, about the question that had so exercised him in prison: how can we find a way of working together and trusting each other, instead of opposing and hurting each other?

I remember how we grappled with this, and think of it frequently now, as we watch trust leaking away from our own society. The reasons for this are complex, of course, but one of them must surely be that in a 'global' world nations and societies are bound to break apart. Globalism's advantages are obvious – for instance, we can live in one country and work in another; we can co-operate, if we so choose, to limit the damage we do to our planet. But there is also a terrible loss of context – and with it the capacity to trust.

Without context, neighbours very often never even learn each other's names, and may seldom put themselves out for each other. Without trust, nothing is reliably done on a nod or a handshake as it was, for instance, in the case of my friend Henri Schoup, a Belgian journalist posted for two years to his news agency's London office in the late 1960s .

As an unnaturalised alien, he was required by law to 'sign in' weekly at the local police station. This became frustrating and professionally inconvenient, so Henri wrote to the Home Office to find out if any other option was available. The following Sunday afternoon there was an unexpected knock at the door.

The caller explained he was from the Home Office, and asked to come in. A couple of hours of tea, cake and pleasant conversation later, he left. At the door he thanked Henri and his wife, and said to Henri: "I am happy to tell you that from now on you may consider yourself a guest of Her Majesty's Government."

This is now unthinkable. Because trust and context have since then largely disappeared, and with it this kind of flexibility and informal sophisticated assessment, our culture has become one of suspicion, blame and regulation. It's as if people with no knowledge or experience of what's involved were passing laws and edicts telling pilots precisely how they must fly. Unsurprisingly, the result is usually a crash.

Blanket regulation means, for example, that doctors can no longer do what they have done for generations: at the right moment, with few words spoken, ease a patient's passing. That was something taken for granted when doctors had built a relationship of trust with their patients over years, and made home visits as a matter of course. But a single Harold Shipman has resulted in measures causing a body of largely competent and compassionate professionals constantly to watch their backs, unable to make informed choices about how best to help terminally suffering patients, and aware that certain decisions would turn them into criminals.

Indeed, clumsy and inappropriate rules and regulations are applied piecemeal to whole professions. It seems as if the regulators think that any vaguely plausible idea should be jetted onto the statute books. Most tend to show little understanding of context or potential consequences. As Philip Zimbardo wryly commented only weeks before I wrote these words, "no one in history, not even the worst of dictators, thought that what they were doing was wrong or evil rather than just what was necessary". Our culture has held this understanding for centuries, and was expressed (approximately) in the familiar proverbial form as early as Virgil's day: the road to hell is paved with good intentions.

I even remember South African president Hendrik Verwoerd, the ghastly architect of apartheid, holding up a newly designed version of the infamous 'pass' book, by which means the movements of black people were callously regulated and restricted, explaining in kindly, avuncular tones how much their bearers would like them, what with the pleasant new colour, and the new size that would fit in the pocket. And blow me down, I think he thought he meant it.

But regulation and rigid control always force us apart. Trust is what links us. However, if we are not trustworthy ourselves, we will not trust others. I recently heard a lad on the radio explaining the knife culture: "You have to be as violent as you can to someone else before they're violent to you."

Yet only a degraded sense of power comes from violence, which in any case is usually generated by feelings of helplessness, and only limited power comes from wealth and status. If an individual is trusted because others know that the person in question has never harmed them, even if they could have done, that is power of a truly high order. Such people, if they happen to be known publicly, become beacons in their societies.

Perhaps we are suffering the inevitable fate of living in transitional times. After all, our planet has endured many violent upheavals in its past, and so has the life on it. First the sheer physical battering as the earth was banged about and moulded in the furnace of the cosmos into the jewel-like planet it is today. Then came analogous upheavals as life emerged and evolved. Then again, in our own species, as modes of organisation transformed from families into groups, groups into tribes, tribes into nations. Now perhaps we are experiencing the upheaval of our own times, as we begin to transcend geography and live increasingly within networks.

That night with Joe the butcher, we talked in terms of what social changes would be needed to build trust. But now it seems to me that looking for trust in social change might not be the right approach. Trust begins elsewhere – at home, within oneself, nurtured within the family. From there it becomes a two-way street, tested between individuals situation by situation, context by context.

There will probably always be those who think in terms of 'us and them'. But our survival in a global world may well depend on whether enough of us can avoid this, and return to where we began, experiencing ourselves again as part of a family – the global family now. Scientists have very recently confirmed that we all come from the same place, descended from the same small band of humans. So in fact, and in truth, you could say that everyone is 'us'.

49

Ins and outs of
the virtual life

I WAS ONCE in a Land Rover in the African bush, observing a group of rhinos with the driver, the ranger, and three others. At one point two of our number, German tourists clearly unaware that these flesh and blood tanks could charge at us, demanded that the ranger throw a stone at them, so they would look our way and provide better photographs.

I remember, too, a summer on Arran, the inner Hebridean island where I live much of the year, when a 43-year-old camper came across a nest of adders. He picked up one in each hand, held them high, and invited his companions to take his picture. Unsurprisingly they bit him – a terrifying six times (which the local paper said was a record) and he fell unconscious. In the nick of time, as in all good adventure stories, the rescue helicopter arrived and flew him to hospital on the mainland. Lucky man. Against the odds his life was saved.

But wasn't he aware that some snakes are deadly? Did he think that acting like a TV wild life presenter meant he *was* one? Didn't he realise that these people are schooled in their subjects and their jobs are dangerous? (A point grimly made just a fortnight later, when Steve Irwin, the Australian wildlife expert known as 'the crocodile hunter', was stabbed in the heart by a sting ray.)

Perhaps the real danger is, in fact, that if we only experience the natural world on a TV screen, passively, in perfect safety, then though that world seems to be very familiar, when we go there in real life we are inexperienced, unaware of dangers and consequences.

Drenched as we are in digital information, the virtual and the real have a dangerous way of changing places behind our backs – and not only in the natural world. A doctor friend told me about a teenage gang member nicked by a bullet complaining to him how painful it was. "What did you expect?" said my friend. "You've been shot." "Well I didn't know it *hurt*," said the aggrieved youth.

Single men and women, young and not so young, give themselves the illusion of a social life while never leaving their own rooms, 'meeting' and flirting with cyber individuals, without needing to interact with all the things the virtual chat leaves out – their awkward humanity, their limitations, their faults, their smells and habits. Indeed a whole employment industry in the real world has developed to earn virtual 'valuables' for computer game maniacs, for whom winning is all that matters, and playing the actual game is tedious.

There are whole digital worlds out there now, 'metaverses' built and owned by their 'residents'. At the time of writing, *Second Life* was probably the best known of them, with its own economy and currency, the L$, (Linden dollar). Members bought land and did business, earning their money by selling objects or services within the virtual environment. According to *Popular Science*, in September 2006 through currency trading, shopping and land sales, *Second Life* had a GDP of L$64 million, and some of its virtual enterprises had streamed from the screen and been downloaded into the real world.

Sadly, as we have seen, even war is waged digitally these days, often directed by people as much as thousands of miles away, who need never experience the agony of civilians killed and maimed by 'warriors' soaring high above the war and insulated by screens from the reality.

As the boundaries blur, the real world itself can sometimes seem to exist simply for our entertainment. A few years ago I was desperately struggling to keep hold of a man I saw just about to throw himself off Waterloo Bridge, and called across to three women standing nearby to run for the river police. "Oh no, we're just watching" they explained, equably, as if this were an understandable social option. We are all like Chance the gardener now, the Peter Sellers character in the film *Being There,* who when confronted by hoodlums literally pointed the TV remote control at them to switch them off – or at least change the channel.

But willy-nilly, we really *do* live in a virtual world. As many readers know, there is a split-second gap between the brain activity associated with any decision and our conscious awareness of actually making it. And as well as that, imagination itself, that "amplitude of mind" as Wordsworth called it, is constantly creating virtual worlds. Night and day, we go back and forth, in and out, of these virtual states, which are generally known as 'trance' states. Human creativity in all its glory, indeed human evolution itself, depends on this capacity. Art, literature, metaphor, analogy, all are simulations of a virtual world, where we see things 'as if', and are utterly convinced by them at the time our 'entranced' focus is on them – a thought which leads inevitably to the astonishing understanding that if this is so, then we ourselves are virtual, too – metaphors, perhaps.

It seems that whatever we consistently tell ourselves determines what we will experience. For example, neuroscience now confirms that pessimistic 'self talk' prejudices health, while an optimistic focus, even if unrealistic, can make for health, happiness – and also luck. Whether our reactions are virtual or real, originating from galaxies deep and dark within us or from the visible cosmos outside, our brains will always try to bring about what we focus on. We will see what we have selected our attention to see, and miss the rest. Given that split second gap, perhaps we shouldn't be too surprised.

Even day-to-day reality is a learned consensus, an agreement to see some things in a certain way while ignoring other things. Stratton's classic experiment in the 1890s, in which he wore special lenses which inverted what he saw, provides 'an instance worth a thousand', because in spite of his eyes at first seeing everything upside down, very soon they had adjusted, and he was once again seeing perfectly 'normally'.

As digital worlds proliferate, we probably need to remind ourselves to keep plugging our experience back into day-to-day reality, testing what is true in the outside world we share. In psychosis, the virtual is mistaken for the real. So perhaps the salient difference between a Goethe and a madman may be that Goethe made extraordinary journeys through the virtual, imagined, or dream world and then returned to day-to-day reality, expressing his inner experience in an outward form and thereby earthing it. The madman, however, will try to negotiate the outside world while remaining resident in the dream.

If we are not clear about those boundaries we risk ending up like the woman who wants a photo of her late husband copied and retouched. She asks whether the hat her husband is wearing can be erased, because she's always hated it. "Certainly", says the photo shop assistant, "What colour was your husband's hair?" "You'll see when you take the hat off", says the woman.

When computers first arrived on the scene, some thinkers warned that those who relied on them for their inner lives would themselves be turned into machines. And 20 years or so on, here we are, increasingly the unwitting creatures of machines which so deplete our compassion, intuition, judgement, discrimination, and even our instinct for self-protection, that we blithely delude ourselves that we are unassailable and invincible – able to pick up poisonous snakes with impunity.

50

Putting our
house in order

IT SEEMS to me that living in our world at present is like living in a large, very badly run house.

I can almost hear the owners complain. "You can't get a decent class of servant these days." "They lack life experience." "They're total skivers!" Or more: "they're thieves, liars, cheats, hypocrites, wilfully blind, trumpeting braggarts, or just plain stupid. They're also *so* self-important they think they deserve huge wages. On top of which, they demand praise and attention too. In fact they are so deluded that they think that we, their employers, should be serving *them*. What a mess!"

Wherever we look in public life, such complaint is frequently borne out. Many, though not all, of those we hire to run our 'house' equate the job with advantage, or power, or profits, or status. To them, 'public service' is a career move – often with a highly lucrative 'revolving door' at the end.

That's not to say such people don't deserve robust recompense for their work, and even the occasional jamboree. After all, they are willing to do a job that *someone* has to do, but which most sane people would want to avoid at all costs. Sadly, however, the wholly honourable head of state, public servant, politician, or even CEO seems to be a vanishing phenomenon – except, that is, for most of the armed servants who guard our 'house', and are prepared to give their lives for it if necessary.

As it happens, I know a lot about good servants – enough to be aware that in essence there is no difference between a truly good servant and a truly good human being. Having grown up in apartheid South Africa, a society in which all white families employed black servants, I learned this at our servants' knees. Their gifts to me were beyond price. They did their jobs well, for cruelly miserly pay, the norm in those days – and as an invisible extra, the two women my parents employed as cook and housemaid probably saved my life. In our frigid and unhappy household, they extended towards me the warmth and humanity that was absent in my family environment but I am sure present in their own. Let me honour them with their names. Adelaide Tembo and Nancy Mgcina, and I love them to this day.

I saw too, how they observed our family, and other white people, from 'underneath', and because they had nothing to gain, clearly understood what we were like. They could mimic us with wicked accuracy, and they forgave all. To them, human service was extended as naturally, and as without question, as breathing. Had they been faced, as we in Europe currently are, with refugees fleeing war zones, I think they would probably have shared whatever they had, however little that was.

It was through Adelaide and Nancy that I began to learn that real service is given willingly, without even the awareness of doing so – simply in response to a need, and usually without being asked. And that seems to be the nub of it. It's part of being human. Service is not a 'job' so much as a function – an invisible responsibility within (and even without!) any job.

For instance, years ago my husband David was at a crowded bus station in Casablanca, and gave some of his loose change to a woman who was begging there. He then went on to buy his ticket, only to find he was a couple of coins short of the required amount. In fact, it wasn't all that serious, as he had more funds stowed away in his money belt. But before he could even think of that, and was still fumbling in his pocket, the beggar woman suddenly materialised at his side, handed back the precise amount he needed, and then disappeared into the crowd again.

However, I can see on reflection that a strong desire or compulsion to serve negates its proper functioning, because it both brings with it an element of 'performance' and 'do-goodery' and also requires gratitude in return — thereby damaging both giver and receiver. Hence the traditional injunction to 'do good by stealth'. Obviously many examples remain hidden, but here's one we finally found out about. On the eve of the Second World War, British stockbroker Nicholas Winton organised the rescue from Czechoslovakia of 669 children, most of them Jewish. From his 'office' – a dining room table in his hotel in Prague – he arranged for safe passage to Britain for each one of them, and also found homes for them all. The world only found out about this over 40 years later – and even then, not directly from him.

When I began writing this page, it was 'public' service I had in mind. But the idea soon broadened into a cluster of associations, among them fairness, empathy, sharing, co-operation, service itself, and altruism, facets of the same jewel, typifying the best of human behaviour. But now we must think again – because research is making it increasingly clear that other mammals demonstrate these qualities too. A chimpanzee given sweet, nourishing grapes has been observed sharing them with another chimp in the next cage, who has been given only cucumber. A rat which has learned it will receive a food reward by pressing the correct lever, will stop pressing it if he sees the rat in the adjacent cage simultaneously getting an electric shock. Such examples seem to share the pattern of behaviour of the woman at the bus station, who clearly did not want to benefit at the expense of David 'losing out'.

Given the growing evidence that mammals are capable of behaving this way, perhaps what should be remarkable is not that she gave back the coins he needed, but that her behaviour was so surprising.

However, I glimpse an interesting distinction. Presumably the whole range of 'altruistic' behaviours in mammals must compete with, and will normally be over-ridden by, more urgent survival needs. But there remains something else, lying perhaps at a level above and beyond these more inherent ones. Its precise nature bears thought, for which I have run out of space here, but it could be called 'true' generosity.

It seems to me that if we are ever to look after our 'house' properly, masters and servants alike need to exercise the whole range of service, from empathy to generosity to unspoken love – which is what my dear friends Adelaide and Nancy gave me every day, unstintingly.

51

A safe place
to learn in

ONE OF THE core imperatives in every human being is the heartfelt need to learn, to solve problems, and to give our best efforts to understanding ourselves, the world we live in, and what we are *for*. Yet both as individuals and as a society, most of us repeatedly act against the reality of those needs, and thus against our hearts' sincere desire.

At other times and in other cultures the fulfilment of the need to learn was the domain of initiation or education – and education's ideal was to produce balanced people, familiar with the culture's knowledge, useful to others, true to themselves. The ideal still kicks around, and also shines within most children – that is, until they actually step inside a school for a few years.

For as most of us are aware, since the industrial revolution society has increasingly disconnected education from concepts of the ideal. And so low have we fallen since then, that a British Prime Minister in 2001 caused few shock waves when he described education as "our number one microeconomic policy" – that is to say, an aspect of the world of business.

In my own schooldays, the requirements of the curriculum were there to be got out of the way as fast as possible, so we could return to what the teacher thought really worth learning. But teachers today have less room for manoeuvre. Even the rare, unsung and dedicated educators, whose vocation in life is to teach, can hardly cope with the load. As well as serving a demanding curriculum, they are caught in the ever-expanding tentacles of bureaucracy and form-filling, and are expected to be social workers as well. Meanwhile schools' 'performance' – a word which should not be allowed anywhere near the word education – is determined by league tables and external observation. Yet our ability to think, to appreciate music or read a book simply cannot be understood or measured from outside.

So how can we create an atmosphere in which young people can aspire to a path more satisfying, more in line with their true heart's desire, than job, money, clothes, clubs, and as much sex as can be found?

Over the years, I've entertained myself dreaming up a number of wheezes. The first, years ago, was for a kind of National Service, in which selected individuals would be called upon, towards the end of their lives rather than in youth, to make themselves available in a school. And by simply being there, sitting about, chatting whenever anyone wanted to talk to them, building rapport and communicating what they had done and learned in their lives, they would expand the horizons of the children they met.

The second was a scheme which a friend and I prepared and researched in our local area, and then handed over to an appropriate agency. They professed themselves delighted with it, assured us they would take it forward – then put all the documentation in a cupboard and promptly lost it when they moved.

The idea had been for an Association for the Recycling of Know-how, with the handy acronym of ARK, in which older people could either do, or demonstrate how to do, jobs for younger people in their area. Someone who knew how to make children's clothes, for example, might offer to make them for a busy mother, or teach her how to make them herself. A retired entrepreneur could either supervise or advise a group of young adults with a project.

The intention was to feed back know-how and skills into society, with the bonus of fostering friendships or at least social contact, between young and old, as well as diluting the feelings of isolation or worthlessness in many of the elderly, and helping them earn a little extra cash. (Incidentally, it says something about how we spend our lives that most of the retired people on our books offered to share expertise not from their jobs but from their hobbies. For example, the woman who offered to make clothes had been a senior civil servant.)

The third wheeze was the result of my observing, years ago, how well children learned, and were motivated to learn, when proper education was officially forbidden – as it was in apartheid South Africa. The result was the creation of hidden, 'secret schools', some of which I was privileged to see. So my current idea is for a subversive education 'underground', through which dedicated education 'patriots' would fight the encroaching barbarian culture. There would be at least one undercover agent in every school – a particular teacher who would spot the child hungry for more in any particular subject, whether maths, literature, history or science. And in circumstances of the utmost secrecy they would slip the child an address. "Be there at 3pm next Tuesday," the teacher might whisper. "Knock three times and ask for David. Memorise the address, then burn it."

And all over the country there would be Davids waiting in educational 'safe houses', special agents able to receive and teach their selected, secret pupils.

And now here is my latest wheeze. Sometimes the place where therapy is done can be a 'safe house' too. Particularly now that therapy's ideologies are falling away, and being replaced by a set of practical techniques and strategies – tools which when used with creative perception can often help our 'students' remove the obstacles blocking their paths.

For instance, therapy clients are partly disadvantaged, as we all have been, by the inheritance of a number of disabling mental postures from the culture, which emphasises certain things at the expense of others, and currently infects us all with pessimism. And they will have been affected, too, by a family culture which does exactly the same.

What is more, children's strongest imperative is to survive into adulthood if possible and in order to do so they must become masters of whatever strategies and tactics they deem necessary. Inevitably this will be at the expense of their full potential.

In the therapy session, however, we can try to help clients discover that they have a wider range of options than they imagine: that they can develop a flexibility of thought which will generalise beyond the specific difficulty the therapy is addressing. We can attempt to fill in gaps in their understanding, showing them how to disentangle certain things they think are the same but are really different, and others that they think different but are really the same. We can give them information, share our knowledge, lend them books. And above all, we can help them develop the confidence to move forward towards their heart's desire. To me, that all sounds like the essence of education.

52

The real cost
per word

YEARS AGO I was hired by CBS TV in America to write a documentary about the journeys of Odysseus. Lines from the *Odyssey* would obviously have to be quoted in such a script – but the film's director, a brash American with bright yellow-dyed hair, was determined not to pay for them.

The author of the translation we wanted to use was E.V. Rieu, who was also the editor of Penguin Classics. "Go and see him", the director ordered. "He's old. Talk him into giving us the lines for nothing."

The 'old man', with whom I instantly fell in love, along with his wife, turned out to be so unworldly that he probably *would* have let us use his words for free. But I was determined to protect him. I told the director that I had found Rieu very fierce, that he was already suing a newspaper which had pinched some of his lines, and that if we were to keep him sweet I should immediately buy him a present. Then thus suitably softened up, I could see what was the least he would be prepared to accept.

In the end I got Mr Rieu a decent sum, but not before the director had suggested I find all the extant translations, read them, and then cobble together a version of my own. That way we wouldn't need to pay anyone anything.

Because the boorish director pictured Mr Rieu as a frightening intellectual and university don, he was too scared to meet him, so had to rely on what I told him about our encounters. As a result, Mr Rieu received both his gift (a fossil starfish embedded in slate) and a decent payment. And I gained a family friendship with the Rieu family, which lasted the rest of their lives.

But why was the director so obstinately reluctant to pay, given the sum was by far the smallest item in his whopping budget? Indeed why are there always so many examples of people grabbing free rides on writers' backs? Close to home, for instance, my husband David has had his own work picked up and published in other countries without either his knowledge or permission. And a close friend of mine, who pioneered and developed for our times the idea of 'natural' beauty, and also brought massage out of the shadows and into its eminence today, had the text of her first book stolen virtually word for word in America. As well as that, a notable British celebrity career was built by an individual who hijacked that same friend's work and passed it off as her own. And now, though to a much lesser extent, it has happened to me. I have had to pay someone else for words I wrote myself.

Many decades ago I wrote the original book and lyrics for South Africa's first-ever musical called *King Kong*, (not the gorilla but a heavyweight boxer). It broke all theatrical records, changed the lives of everybody connected with it, propelled a number of our cast to international fame, and over the years achieved an almost mythical status in South Africa. When with much fanfare it was revived nearly 60 years later, I wrote a memoir of the original show, and quoted some of my songs in it.

In my innocence, I assumed that because the lyrics came out of my own head, I owned the rights to them. But to my astonishment, the copyright actually belonged to a large music publisher, who was asking £300 for each song or part thereof. Then 'because I was the author', the sum was magnanimously halved. Ultimately I bargained them down to £50 per song, but that still meant, for instance, that a very short quote from one of the songs ended up costing me £5.00 for each of my own words.

I had reckoned with the prospect of deletions for legal reasons – which unfortunately lost a lot of the memoir's true stories illustrating the iniquities of apartheid. But I was *not* expecting how the freelance copy editor appointed by the publishers removed all traces of my 'voice' from the text and, shockingly, edited the life out of it. She also made weird arbitrary changes, as if she were the ghost writer of a book of her own devising. And this was after the text had been brilliantly and insightfully edited by Denise Winn, who is also editor of the *Human Givens* Journal. It should have gone through on the nod, except for changes into the publisher's house style. Instead, it required a hell of a lot of work to repair the damage.

Such savage editorial 'appropriation' is surprisingly common, so I hear from many writers. A scientist friend says that even in his world, editors ignore the scientists' personal voice and homogenise their texts to make them more acceptable – "more plain vanilla", in his words, "for some broader audience of their imaginations". And I suppose, too, that in a society where 'appearances' dominate, many editorial marks on each page can be taken as evidence of work carefully and lengthily done. Indeed early in my career, temporarily a book editor myself, I came across a work so perfectly constructed and written that I refused to change a word of it – as a result of which, I was fired for not doing my job.

Of course none of this may matter much to individuals uninvolved in the writing world. But the patterns of thought and behaviour I have been describing have, I think, wider and deeper implications. Probably the majority of us are at times covert thieves and hypocrites, stealing anything we can get away with that gives us an advantage, or makes us look good, or saves us work. And word-stealing (together with the ideas they carry) is among the easiest thefts – and easy to justify too, because we all use words anyway. So an author's words can't really count as their 'property', can they? Unlike, say, a bag of sugar, they have no material value. Once words are 'out there', it's as if they had always been there. Why pay for them then, if we can get away with not?

But in the long run, of course, we don't get away with it. Robbing an author of both payment and acknowledgement of their work, is not only theft but also sheer lack of generosity – and lack of generosity is one of the factors which keeps us in our mental prisons.

Certainly I see in myself precisely the habits I've been describing. Too many times, in domains well beyond the written word, the greed in me will hijack decent behaviour, the thief in me will appropriate the ideas of others, and the laziness in me will take shortcuts and obstruct the real and necessary effort of thinking for myself. And the cost of that, to me, as indeed to any of us who do this kind of thing, is a great deal more than £5 a word.

53

All in the
family

SOME YEARS ago I was commissioned by *The Times* to write a feature article on cults, based on an interview with an acquaintance of mine, American psychiatrist Arthur Deikman. Deikman, author of *The Observing Self*, had made a study of cult behaviour, and I had found what he said illuminating and useful. The features editor of *The Times*, however, did not. "There's nothing in it," he said, "nothing of any interest at all."

His response didn't altogether surprise me, because I'd found before that ideas which came too close for comfort, which could not be held at sufficient distance to elicit a reader's gee-whizz or tut-tut response, and which were written in a neutral, unemotional tone, were almost always said to have 'nothing' in them. This denial in itself displays one crucial ingredient of cultic thinking – a closed mind. And it's one not confined, of course, to the press.

First let me recapitulate some of what Deikman had said. He talked about how in the early 1980s, when he was clinical professor of psychiatry at Berkeley University, a nuclear war seemed a distinct possibility. He was a member of Physicians for Social Responsibility at the time, and wondered what, if anything, could be salvaged from a nuclear catastrophe. He did some research, and found that a nuclear war would probably leave more than a hundred million US survivors – who might have a much better chance if adequate food and sheltering could be organised. "So it seemed to me logical," he told me, "that while working in every way one could to prevent nuclear war, we should also think about protecting those left alive."

But when he told these ideas to his peace movement friends he saw their eyes narrow and their faces tighten. "He's a civil defencer!" their expression seemed to signify. "How can he be saying this?" "It was as though they were reaching into their heads and taking my name from the 'good guys' file and putting it in the 'bad guys' file," said Deikman. "None of them asked, 'Why do you think that?' They just closed ranks and rejected me."

Thus it was he found out what it was like to be exposed to the righteous rejection of the 'good' people – and realised how often he had responded in this same way to others. "It was quite a shock. I thought my satisfying feelings of righteousness could be relied on!"

Shortly after this, his experience found a context. He joined a group of eminent psychiatrists, psychologists and sociologists in an ongoing study group on cults, and interviewed cult survivors of all kinds. And he found that no matter their educational or economic level, their stories were strikingly the same.

He noticed, too, that as they described the pressures and distortions "they all seemed vaguely familiar to me. I could get flashes: oh yeah. I know that – I've experienced some of that."

In fact it seemed to him that what they were talking about was not distinctly different from what went on in his own life, or in society at large – it was simply a highly condensed version of day-to-day processes. Cults, he thought, are somehow drawing upon processes that are taking place all the time and making them more intense, so that they are a sort of exaggerated mirror of society.

His research revealed four principal dynamics operating within a cult: 'compliance with a group', 'dependence on a leader', 'avoiding dissent' and 'devaluing the outsider'. He looked at other sectors of society to see if these were present, and lo and behold he found a continuum from the mildest and most open humanistic group possible to a Jonestown commune or a Branch Davidian sect at the far extreme.

This, it seems to me, is a finding of the greatest importance and relevance to us all, for the continuum of cult behaviour is not, of course, restricted to religious groups. When Deikman followed up his hypothesis and looked at material on large corporations, government, and even his own field of psychiatry, he found abundant evidence of the identical processes there too. Such an approach changes the often asked question "is this or that group a cult?" into something far more useful: "How much cult behaviour is present in any group?"

This is the key question, and one which we need to ask ourselves about any group we are involved in. For though people in extreme cults seem very different from the rest of us, it really is only a matter of degree. People may enter a cult with idealistic motives, but once in, other dynamics come into play. This, says Deikman, is because our basic model is the family, families are necessarily authoritarian (a child really does need to be protected and told what to do), and while in a good family you have authority appropriately delegated, in a cult the model becomes some kind of super-family-in-the-head – a mummy and a daddy somewhere above us telling us that if we are good we will be rewarded and if bad then punished.

"Our wishes for security and happiness tend to concretise in some form of family," says Deikman. "It's very hard to think outside that structure, in religions or in daily life. But in order to maintain the fantasy of the ideal family, you have to distort reality. In fact the main cost of cult behaviour is loss of realism, because anything – from independent thought to outsiders presenting different opinions – may shatter the illusion."

In his clear and telling book on cults*, one of the best I've read, Deikman points out how cult leaders infantilise their members within this constructed family (many cults even call themselves 'the family'), offering security in exchange for an individual's autonomy. All totalitarian structures mobilise this family image (which explains all those huge pictures of the 'beloved leader') but so, to a lesser degree, does our own army, our government, and political, professional and working structures. For in ordinary life too, adults as well as children must consciously and unconsciously preserve the good opinion of the person or people on whom they are dependent.

And once this happens our minds are very adaptive. It's not as if we say, "Well, I don't dare say this to my boss/teacher/superior, because I will be fired/passed over for promotion/ostracised." At first we may feel that and even talk about it as a problem. But if we feel we need to remain within the organisation, soon even the thought stops coming up.

We can easily see this internalised and unconscious toeing the line and lack of dissent in politics, for instance, where authority may devalue the outsider by withholding information, even in situations

---

* *The Wrong Way Home: Uncovering the Patterns of Cult Behaviour in American Society* A.Deikman, 1990

which have nothing to do with technical or special knowledge. Or where party members in good standing turn insufficiently useful or faithful insiders into outsiders by means of malicious rumours and 'leaks'. In the media, too, as I know from experience, people tune themselves into the wavelength of the organisation, and seldom have their work rejected (as my piece was), because they simply don't submit material that would run into that problem.

Therapy itself, with its hundreds of schools, is also riddled with cult behaviour. Deikman found it in his own field of psychiatry, and it is also noticeably strong, of course, in Freudian psychoanalysis. We are sufficiently distant now to see it for what it is: a formidable system of brainwashing with a hierarchical structure and a potent system of succession.

Deikman mentioned, as one example of this, a sociological study which found that in spite of systems in place for the training analysts to select candidates to the profession, the actual selection was informal and covert – power being wielded by an in-group of third parties. "Someone could mention the candidate's name, and the other person could raise their eyebrows, and that's all it would take." Jungian psychoanalysis, too, can be seen as a cult: and has, indeed, been described in *The Jung Cult* by Richard Noll (Princeton 1995). His analysis of the present-day cult and its disciples, which sprang almost inevitably from Jung's own *völkisch* ideology, is in many respects truly devastating.

Similarly, counsellors and therapists know the stranglehold that cultic elements can have on trainees. In my own training, many questions were implicitly 'forbidden'. The more sincere or innocent they were, the more our tutors seemed to respond to them with a subtle or not-so-subtle sneer or put-down. The implication was: "You are not one of us", and behind that lay a more menacing implication: "and if you keep on like this you never will be". I remember the knowing smirks that passed between compliant students and teachers when one of us, and often it was me, would say something clearly not 'on message'. "Fool," those smirks implied, "you'll fail unless you change your tune."

For instance, I remember once asking, as delicately as I could, whether it was possible that symptoms might remit by means of other techniques, without a therapist needing to dig so exhaustively into a client's past. My tutor said darkly: "If I were you, I'd think very carefully about why you asked that question." Saying, in effect: "Oh, miserable sinner, don't even think you can think for yourself. Stay in the ranks of the obedient."

We've all, I imagine, been on both sides of the fence. I've found myself defensive and touchy, deserted by my sense of humour, when someone challenges or rides roughshod over one of my cherished beliefs. I've behaved just like that *Times* features editor when faced with a concept too subtle, different, unfamiliar or unemotional to hook onto my existing infrastructure of ideas. I, too, tend to prefer ideas which challenge my own, served up with a generous dollop of emotional persuasion. And emotion, of course, is the fuel of cults.

For instance, if individual A were to say something of the utmost importance that could perhaps ultimately save our lives, and say it in a relaxed and low-key way, and if individual B were to impart a dazzling, emotional message, full of words onto which we project our own meaning like, say, 'fulfillment' or 'progress' or 'fate' or 'democracy', even if B's message would eventually lead to our doom, most of us would not even register the first in the stampede over the nearest precipice at the behest of the second. I cast the idea in the preceding sentence into the future by using the word 'if '. But a pause for thought has shown me the grim truth; this is already happening – and happening as a result of cult-like thinking.

But aren't all groups by their very existence prey to the dynamics of cult behaviour? The answer seems to be yes – in most organisations these dynamics will indeed be present, but at a manageable level. Many of the self-help groups around at present, for example, are not cults. Their membership is wide open, their boundaries totally permeable, their interest in having 'a leader' negligible.

What, then, are the antidotes to cult behaviour? I think they would include:

- Learning that feelings of self-righteousness can't ever be trusted, and in fact are a reliable signal that something is awry. Indeed these feelings are usually a prelude to some of the worst excesses of human beings, including violence. Cults, of course, are permeated with self-righteousness.

- Trying to defuse these feelings of self-righteousness by asking the person who opposes us, with genuine interest: "Why do you think that?"

- Realising that if someone's point of view seems boring or trivial, then it's worth looking to see if we are holding on to a deeply embedded point of view ourselves. Pointers to the fact that we may be doing this are feelings of superiority, touchiness, or irritation.

- Trying to maintain awareness. Once we can spot the cult behaviour, we have more choice, more freedom. In this it is helpful to notice when our sense of humour deserts us. Totalitarian regimes bitterly hate jokes about themselves, because humour will always undermine cult behaviour.

- Understanding that it is possible to communicate pleasantly and neutrally, without attempting to whip up anyone's feelings. The absence of emotion does not mean being callous, cynical or cold.

- Ensuring that we do not put all our eggs in one basket. Without a range and variety of interests, and our needs being met in a variety of ways, we risk becoming dependent on a single individual or organisation.

- And finally, appreciating that we need realism to understand anything – for in reality, there are no outsiders, and there are many ways of seeing things. That is why realism is the first casualty of cult behaviour. In fact it was only by shifting his viewpoint on civil defence that Deikman realised he had been a member of a 'good guy' group with a strong component of cult behaviour. "I'd never have known that," he said, "had I not started challenging their dogma."

And that, I think, is at the heart of it. If we want to be free of as much cult behaviour as possible, we must be alert, watchful, and prepared to challenge the dogma of our own 'side'. But to challenge it only as and when necessary, remembering always that there is no easy, mechanical fix. If we become permanently and consistently vigilant against cults, that posture in itself will turn into its opposite – and become, inevitably, cult behaviour.

54

Editing our
home movies

IN RECENT years everyone in the UK has been able to watch the 'EU Leave/Remain' circus acting out a basic piece of human behaviour so blatantly that it served as an object-lesson – how to portray a desired 'reality' by means of selective presentation. When the public inevitably got wise to the blatant spin and began shouting for the facts, the politicians and their advisers simply emphasised that what they were saying *were* the 'facts'.

All very laughable and troubling – but I think no different in kind, and perhaps not even in degree, to what we do with the stories we spin about ourselves. I have realised for decades that what I think of as my life (perhaps you think yours is too) is rather like a film projected from a movie camera – a final edit, with a lot of material left on the cutting room floor.

Not only is it different from the real 'truth' about ourselves, but it is also quite unlike how others are registering us. Indeed, if we could see through their eyes we would hardly recognise ourselves. Therapists and divorce lawyers quickly discover that should they ever meet the spouse of their client, they would find it hard to identify the delightful individual in front of them as the duplicitous or incompetent creature they'd heard so much plausible complaint about.

We are, so it seems to me, masters of 'creative accounting', but the fraud we perpetrate is mainly on ourselves. It's also very hard to spot. Recently, for instance, a client reeled into my therapy room in a state of shock. He had been hearing for years from his wife and friends how judgemental he was; how he looked down on them, and how tangling and hurtful this was. But that was not why he had come. He came because the *consciousness* of this had suddenly presented itself to him like a thunderbolt, painfully overwhelming him for several days and nights thereafter. But in fact, of course, this was a 'gift' – he had finally been able to see an aspect of himself usually left on the cutting room floor, and it could only have been because some part of him, at last, was ready to. The therapeutic task, as I saw it, was to help him gratefully accept the experience and move forward.

The capacity to hide our limitations probably begins as a survival mechanism – a strategy to keep us going when we meet an obstacle in this often taxing world we find ourselves in. However if the strategy is not soon dropped it becomes pervasive, adding another 'blind spot' to the already distorted 'edited version', and slowing down our development and understanding.

Much of the editing is, of course, fashioned by 'consensus society', presumably because it must be – given that we need to be anchored in the day-to-day world even while our consciousness roams where it will. But unfortunately the consensus turns most of us into what a friend of mine calls 'lookists'. Appearances matter. I like to look unselfish and clever, for instance, because I know I am neither. A friend of mine, who *is* very clever, dissembles so as to seem more like the rest of us, and spends a lot of time on how she looks and dresses, because this is where *she* feels she doesn't measure up. I think we are all 'lookists' of one sort or another, and most of us prefer our friends to look good too. Certainly the culture encourages it, extolling 'individuality' while at the same time moulding us to seem as similar as penguins.

Consensus also writes the script of what 'ought' to be, stoking our expectations of how events should play out. If a partner or child suddenly disappears, for example, or a friend is murdered, or the house burns down, the mind tries to tell us, over and over again, that it hasn't happened, that it was all a mistake, that it's not true. Paradoxically, our 'unscripted' events, whether tragic or joyous, can make real experience seem utterly *un*real.

Many writers know the injunction of Robert Graves, that "you must be able to murder your little darlings". These are the phrases, paragraphs or sections which block the path of the intended communication – usually the bits one likes best, feels are essential, and would never cut. But only after reluctantly chopping them from the text can one see that the 'darling' had too much of our ego invested in it. Perhaps it makes us look clever, or represents weeks of research, or we are in love with our admirably poetic description, or our perceptive or knowledgeable observation. But only once these are removed can real work proceed.

We 'lookists' find it just as difficult to edit our life's little darlings. They hide out of our awareness, and our gaze slides over them, just as the writer's does. I remember an intrepid friend who wanted to become 'a better person' – and decided that her chief failing was lack of courage. She hated swimming, was terrified of water, so she spent months learning to scuba dive. But any observer could see that a good scuba diver was not the same as 'a better person'.

Observation, in fact, is a brilliant mirror which helps us detect what we may have 'edited' so as to seem like 'better' people. Indeed we lookists can learn a lot simply by watching others similarly afflicted. My scuba-diving friend, for instance, probably needed to make *less* effort, but in another direction – where doubtless she would have found a number of little darlings lurking in the shadows.

The 'edited movie', however, seems to be a pattern also rooted in our biology. We know that incoming stimuli are processed unconsciously before being transferred to the conscious mind, and until recently it was thought that this information streamed continuously into consciousness. But recent research suggests that it is not a smooth uploading but a two-stage process: information from the environment is processed unconsciously, and when unconscious processing is 'completed' a series of 'snapshots' are "simultaneously rendered conscious at discrete moments in time". So here too, we can talk of elements left on the cutting room floor. It seems that the huge territory of potential consciousness is edited as well, and few of us know what would be revealed were we to become aware of the whole of the ground in which living things are immersed.

55

Patronising? Well
yes, I am...

ONE OF the cornerstones of today's political correctness is the unquestioning abhorrence of the attitude characterised as 'patronising'. It is invariably viewed as – here's another buzzword – 'disempowering'.

"Don't patronise me!" growls the teenager, when his omniscience/omnipotence is, however obliquely, put into question. However, given the gap in experience between myself and the aforementioned young grub, the 'patronising' mental posture can be seen as reflecting the true state of affairs. "My dear child," I am sometimes tempted to say, "Even though female, in any relationship we enter into I am your patron and sponsor – or at very least I am *in loco parentis*. You may not like the fact, but if you ignore it you will remain stuck right where you are, bogged down in your own subjective unreality."

In psychotherapy it is axiomatic that the therapist is the client's 'patron'. In education too, whatever the curriculum, the teacher-pupil relationship surely presupposes that a course of study begins with the teacher 'patronising' the student, and ends when he no longer needs to do so.

A friend who is a former language teacher, and a very good one, tells me: "When a pupil says something like: *la livre est sur le table*, I don't jump in with: "No, you blithering idiot, it's: *LE livre est sur LA table*. That would be a total turn-off. What kind of a conversation could possibly evolve on those lines?

"So I merely respond conversationally to the actual truth and relevance (or otherwise) of the utterance, insofar as I have understood it, echoing where possible what my student actually meant in a more correct form: *Oui, c'est ça: le livre est sur la table.*

"Such redundant echoing", he continues, "is in any case a normal feature of most languages, so that the correction of the form can take place unobtrusively without the thread of content and context being broken. The pupil will notice that this has happened, and also that in a certain sense he or she is being 'humoured'.

"You can call that patronising if you like: I call it teaching. And when, next time, the pupil uses the correct pattern, the motivational feedback loop will be completed, as he or she experiences the pleasurable sensation of aligning themselves with an unconscious cultural norm."

It seems to me that part of the trouble arises from a mistaken perception of what knowledge and learning really are. We tend nowadays to look on them as commodities, to be quantified and evaluated, bought and sold. I know such-and-such, so pay me, gimme applause, a PhD, a knighthood. You don't know what I know, so I'm worth more than you. If we are told something we already know, we can get quite shirty: "I knew that!" we hiss. Again the message, quite clearly is: "Don't patronise me!" Or else, when confronted with new information, there are those who launch into a half-hour monologue outlining the lamentable history of deprivation and abuse that hitherto has effectively prevented them from knowing it. The actual knowledge, its truth, relevance and value, is lost in a torrent of self-pity.

But in both cases the question of whether or not we knew a certain fact assumes greater importance in our minds than the knowledge itself. However, despite the endless queues of wannabe millionaires for TV quiz shows, the naked and sober truth is that knowledge is its own reward and indeed the only reward of genuine value.

"Because I'm worth it." So runs one of our more obnoxious and, perhaps by that very token, one of our most powerful advertising catchphrases. "Sorry, dear," I long to say, "delightful though you may be in some respects, as long as you think that way you are most decidedly *not* worth it; and anyone who says you are is either a knave or a fool – or wants to sell you something."

But this, of course, is yet another PC shibboleth for the truth is that it is *streng verboten* to say anything that might ever undermine a person's 'self-esteem'. (And by the way even two words in German can be enough for some to cry 'don't patronise me'.)

When I first heard of this mysterious property called self-esteem it puzzled me – having until then always been brought up to regard myself as worthless, a carbuncle on the face of existence. And indeed, this little piece of 'liberation' is possibly the cruellest fraud that has ever been perpetrated on us. It's all very well for us to drift around mouthing the mantra, "I'm worth it, I'm worth it", as the daughter of an old friend recently did while determinedly scrounging a lot of money from me in exchange for a post-dated cheque which bounced. Barely holding her tattered personality together, she wobbled out of my front door in a trance of affirmations that she was strong, that she was wonderful, that she was worth it. Who knows, she may even have succeeded in convincing herself, as any of us may, for a season. But what that poor child actually needed was a strong dose of 'reality', gently administered.

All the while, however, we too are often shirking the serious and immensely fertile question of what 'worth' actually means, what it consists of, where it comes from. And when for one reason or another, the bottom falls out of our world, we are strangely unprepared for the void that engulfs us. A better strategy would surely be to anticipate such reverses from the word go.

Being patronised doesn't usually bother me. I certainly get my share of it – much of it these days from people many years my junior. But there is generally more to be gained – and learned – from rolling with it than from bridling at it. I do not think I can be the only person in the world who is never happier, lighter, more euphoric than when I remember and acknowledge my own nothingness. It is a state of mind the delights of which I try, whenever possible, to tempt my clients to experience. Sometimes I tell them the story of how, in Homer's *Odyssey*, Ulysses evades the giant Cyclops, who has imprisoned him and his men, finally managing to escape because at the crucial moment, when the half-blind Cyclops asks "who's there?", Ulysses is able to say: "I am nobody!" Indeed one of my favourite quotes is: "Fancy yourself no longer there; then smile."

Robert Graves received scant recognition and even less thanks for his version of *Omar Khayaam*. But if he had mined just this single line, and nothing more, his efforts would in my view have been truly 'worth it'.

56

When 'silly'
makes sense

PLAY, AS we know, makes individuals grow up, and the world go round. Like other prerequisites for human survival, the essence of childhood play, and the delight in it, can last a lifetime. Indeed play bubbles up again, together with that delight, whenever we are in love, returning us to the laughter and purity of our early days on earth.

So I have been delighted to come across a book which has helped open the door back to my own childhood – which, though certainly never shut, could still have been more widely ajar. The author is Canadian poet JonArno Lawson, and after reading his new book, entitled *But It's So Silly*, my head is banging about with childhood rhymes and sounds and surmises and insights and memories – and all the accompanying energy, optimism and joy which they bring.

Lawson's book is a cross-cultural collection of nonsense, play and poetry. For the past decade, he has been collecting children's poetry, lap rhymes, finger games and stories of how people interact with young children across the world. The book's blurb summarises: "In this wide-ranging collection we learn of language play from Malta, round games from Jamaica, Yiddish hand rhymes, and of the wonderful and complex ways these are all passed down through generations."

Lap rhymes and finger games, of course, were among the many bridges and walkways over which we travelled early in life, as we mapped our bearings in the unfamiliar world we'd arrived in. They enabled us to explore it through the safety nets of rhythm, rhyme, and silly play, all of which made each new day a wonder and delight.

Although Lawson is mostly thought of as a children's poet (and, happily, he is a very successful one) his work is of a kind that in my opinion no right-thinking adult can resist – light, witty, loving,

sparkling, nonsensical, often philosophical, funny, punny, paradoxical, jokey. But above all, his words trigger *thinking*. Behind
everything he writes, are *ideas*. For instance:

> "I'm trying to recall your face
> I haven't managed yet
> Why are half-remembered things
> The hardest to forget?"

It's a verse children can wonder at, pithy and memorable in itself,
but to me is also resonant of the beautiful biblical psalm, in which
the broken-hearted author plaintively wonders how to sing the
Lord's song in a strange land.

One of the stories Lawson tells in his book struck me with
particular force. When he was a child, he says, he realised that a tune
popularized by Mozart had the same melody as *Twinkle, Twinkle,
Little Star, Baa, Baa, Black Sheep*, and the 'ABC' alphabet song.
Each was so important and completely distinct, he says, so "how
was it possible they all shared a tune, and that it took me so long to
notice this?"

It was a connection that came to mind again years later, after his
father had a stroke. When he got to the hospital, he says, he found
his father alert, but unable to speak, and looking terrified.

A few hours later, Lawson's brother Stephen arrived. He is a
multi-disciplinary artist, and Lawson thinks this occupation may
have been at least partially relevant to what followed.

"As soon as he came in and took in the fact that our father
couldn't speak, he went over to the side of the hospital bed, took his
hand and started to sing to him 'A-B-C-D-E-F-G.' He said later that
he had no idea why he did this. It could be he just had an instinct to
try soothing him with a childhood melody." But perhaps, Lawson
speculates, it had to do with his years of stage work, through which,
without even realising it, he had developed a cohesive sense of how
mind, memory, movement, voice and body all worked seamlessly
as one.

"My father said it was as if he was at the bottom of a dark well,
and someone threw down a ladder. Just like that, out of the silence
the stroke had imposed on him hours before, he started singing
along with my brother.

"He looked startled. We all laughed with relief. And then they kept singing together – the rest of 'ABCs,' then *Baa, Baa, Black Sheep,* then *Twinkle, Twinkle* – the same melody scaffolding all three sets of lyrics. My father's speech was back. He crawled back to language on the alphabet song, as provided, providentially, by my brother at exactly the right moment."

Lawson admits his father might have regained his speech in any case. But on the other hand, the ladder Stephen threw him, along with his love, affection, and *touch,* may have been vital. Perhaps, Lawson speculates, one of the actual functions of nursery rhymes and songs is that they act as an early bridge between sound, rhythm and language. It certainly seems that way to me. Indeed I have a strong feeling that within his compelling story there is a great deal waiting to be understood.

These days, captives as we are to screens, and to the implacable logics of the digital world, there has been (probably in reaction) a surge of hunger for stories about other dimensions and abundant possibilities. This may account in part for the stratospheric success of the stories told by J.K. Rowling and Philip Pullman. In their different ways, they have opened a door to a time in our childhoods, and a place in our minds, when we just *knew* that the world was more, and the world was other. And I think the delicate magic of Lawson (a seeker on a higher plane than these others, so it seems to me) speaks to that same hunger and opens the same door.

That door, of course, rejoins us not only to our childhood, but to all the civilisations and cultures that came before us, every one of which made space for the mysterious, and named that space as sacred. I doubt whether there are small children anywhere in the world who, had they the vocabulary, would disagree. In fact, I've just looked up the etymology of the word 'silly', and discovered to my delight that in earlier centuries it meant 'happy,' 'prosperous' and 'blessed'.

57

Running away
with the circus

THE LAST time I went to the circus I was about twelve, I think, but the impact of its rich sensory attractions remain vivid in my memory. Even before entering the circus tent there was the smell and sound of lions and elephants and horses, of candy floss, grass and chips, and the sight of all the circus folk in or near their caravans, busy in their different ways, preparing for the show. It was so ravishing that my senses would melt; my consciousness seemed almost altered. But above all, what made it so exciting was the feeling of *connectedness* – everyone working together to keep the show on the road and make the enchantment inside the circle of the Big Top come together at the appointed moment. It seemed to trigger some hidden memory I couldn't quite catch hold of.

Spellbinding as the actual show was, however, it was the whole *concept* that lit me up – performers and animals all at their separate tasks creating a glorious unity. And underneath all of *that*, making it even more precious, was the knowledge that it was transitory, that it would pack up and leave. There was nothing you could hang on to at the circus. There for a short while, then gone like a dream.

I have sometimes heard the circus used as a metaphor for daily life, but I think this is not quite right. Instead, it seems to me to be a metaphor for a more *real* life, not the robotic imitation of it most of us find ourselves living out much of the time. And I think this is why so many children, including myself when young, want to run away and join it. Not yet quite brainwashed into believing that the map of society was the actual *territory*, we instinctively saw the circus as representing how life could and *should* have been. If you arrived for the show early enough, you could hang about outside and watch people stretching canvas or their own bodies, hammering, sewing, cooking, rehearsing, working out, exercising the animals.

And even in the dying moments the excitement lingered, as for a few pounds the local youth could be cajoled into lending their muscle power for the rapid dismantling of the Big Top.

I also noticed, even as a child, how strong and 'equal' all the *women* were – and had been for far more than a century, I discovered subsequently – well before the suffrage campaign or the woman's movement was thought of. And, of course, the circus had space for 'marginal' people too, such as its much-valued individuals with dwarfism.

Again, so much of what circus people did was *dangerous*! Coming from our settled, risk-averse suburbs, that thrilled me. Unlike us, circus people were – sometimes literally in the case of sword-throwers and swallowers – living on a knife-edge. And this child in apartheid South Africa marvelled too at the circus's ethnic diversity – as a consequence of which, I recently learned from a BBC radio programme, the circus had developed its own international *lingua franca,* a rich *argot* known as Polari. But elephants, I discovered with delight, are always trained in French.

And then there were the *clowns* – the most popular, as surveys show, of all circus acts. When the modern circus developed in the mid-18th century, clowns were added between equestrian sequences to amuse the spectators. But in fact they are ancient – we know of them in Egypt as far back as 2400 BC, where they traditionally served a psychological and socio-religious role.

Indeed I've learned that among some people, including the Zuni Indians in the United States, the roles of priest and clown have been held by the same person. That makes psychological sense. We need the grotesque distorting mirrors of the clowns just as much as the high aspiration a priesthood is supposed to provide. Clown antics and masked faces display what we are really like when our own masks come off. We see, reflected back to us, exaggerated cartoons of our limitations, mistakes and assumptions. But the message is tolerable, because we can laugh as we wince.

All of us need to be clowns in this life, in fact, prepared to accept slipping on life's banana skins and getting custard pies in our faces. Without that, how would we learn? The trick is to be able to pick ourselves up, rub our bruises, wipe off the custard, and be grateful to whatever brought us down – because mishaps and mistakes are feedback, and thus our teachers. One way or another, I often bring this understanding to therapy clients as a way of detaching them – especially when they seem to be presenting their difficulties over-dramatically.

Of course I know that the circus doesn't appeal to everyone; that it has many critics, and can be seedy, shabby, and cruel to animals. But it is the *essence* of circus which catches me still. Indeed, I recently tried recasting my own life in circus terms, and discovered that my friends are circus people all – jugglers, acrobats, high-fliers, superb riders on life's horses, amazing magicians, wildly brilliant clowns, and even a couple of ring-masters.

One close friend, for instance, is a brilliant illusionist, able to make certain events virtually invisible, so that she can constantly give to others without them quite realising it. Another is a consummate acrobat – somehow managing to stretch herself, and even stretch time, to accommodate everything asked of her. A third, for similar reasons, is a brilliant juggler. Another is tossed from high wire to high wire, and survives with a smile. While my husband David has an almost uncanny capacity to bring dead people back to life. Indeed he spends a lot of his time having fun with his far-flung friends, many of whom left this world centuries ago. Then there are several whose writing skills mesmerise their readers, enabling them to share in lives very different from their own. Magicians, all of them! And among the many others are weight-lifters who can take the heavy human heart and raise it high, such as my beloved friends, singers, dancers, and musicians from South Africa, with whom I have had the privilege of working. And above all, there are the glorious clowns, the lifeblood of the circus – which of course also means the *circle* – of life.

58

Finding everything
in spacetime

A MALE PHEASANT, whom in his successive generations we have come to know as 'Algernon', frequently stalks from the wild field adjacent to our cottage through a space in our rhododendron hedge, continues through our garden towards a gap in the privet hedge which divides us from our neighbours, and thence out of our sight and our story.

Of course for Algernon there are no hedges, gardens and houses, and no stories in which we, the observers from window or raised deck, figure in any way. He is only aware, or so I imagine, of convenient openings which allow him sufficient space to continue on a well trodden path to ... I don't actually know where, because the hedge occludes my view of his progress after he disappears into the neighbours' garden. I presume that the walls of our house and the neighbours' house are sensed as impenetrable, possibly dangerous obstacles from which he keeps his distance. Perhaps they are simply dark or empty blanks in his mental map of the territory. Just as in our minds, too, we have places where we go no further when we sense an implacable obstruction looms near.

The smaller birds, the finches, tits and sparrows, known as passerines, presumably have their own maps too. The rowan tree, just yards from our open deck, is a convenient shaded way-station to perch on, a short flight to the bird feeder hanging over our deck, and a bolt-hole to be quickly accessed if we cast a sudden shadow from our living-room. And whereas the rhododendron hedge is barely a factor for Algernon, who in rare moments of enthusiasm can flutter over it, the hedge is important to the little birds, who use it for their own purposes as a kind of hotel to spend time in, or on, or in the shade of. Occasionally, on specially sunny days, they sunbathe near the edge of that hedge, flat out, wings and tails spread, so that they look like living Klimpt illustrations. It's a charming sight to see a row of them basking in this way. I interpret it as the pleasures of soaking up the sun. Perhaps it is, but from their point of view it may primarily be a way of getting rid of fleas.

Sometimes a black cat turns up and, motionless as stone, watches the birds in the hedge, seeing not so much charm as potential prey. To my knowledge, he has never caught one. But neither the little birds, nor the pheasant, nor the cat, sees what we see when we watch all this going on, in the context of our own labelled boundaries: house, garden, field, steps up to deck (sagely skirted by Algernon), and hedge dividing us from neighbours. Presumably ants and other insects have, at their scale, their own maps too.

So there we are, all of us, intersecting in exactly the same space, in our own realities, within our own maps, for our own purposes. Our minds select and stabilise one or other possible pattern from the ambiguous field which provides us with the forms and patterns of life. In a living-room, I may be tuned to the paintings on the wall, you to the design in the carpet, someone else to the materials, or the relationship between the pieces of furniture, or the view from the window, or even the cooking aromas wafting in from the kitchen. We inhabit the same place, but it may not actually seem so.

As in individuals, so too in human groups. Certain patterns extracted from the field are stabilised into the 'official version', the formal track along which to some extent any society's citizens must perforce agree they are moving through. But if we are to 'get' the whole picture, we need, I think, to be able to let the consensus go from time to time, and drop back into the field. Indeed I can imagine that, in accordance with traditional human beliefs, beings with a much less limited view of where we are, share the same space with the rest of us, unknown and unperceived.

Probably many of us have wondered, as I have, whether it is likely that everyone and everything is inhabiting precisely the same space at the same time – but only conscious of what is relevant within their own maps, scale, purposes and progress, and blind to what else is there? That it is all a matter of interpretation, experience, and the limits of awareness? That even time itself does not exist, but that only a being whose consciousness is able to embrace everything that can be seen will be aware of it all.

Certainly, I have known since childhood that time on its own doesn't really exist, except as an agreed, constructed yardstick, and that it is interchangeable with space. In fact I remember, at the age of 13, arranging to meet a schoolfriend two city blocks away from where we were standing. "I'll see you in two blocks' time", I said, which utterly boggled her, but made perfect sense to me.

It was an instinctive perception I probably shared with many other children also too young to know that it was becoming an accepted concept in physics that yes, everything happens at once, that past, present and future are all equally 'now', that time and space are so inextricably connected that it is even labelled 'spacetime'.

It seems to me that an all-in-one and all-is-one sense of time clarifies many perplexing things including, even, the idea of reincarnation, which has always stuck in my throat. But if everything really is happening at once, then indeed individuals might tap into part of it and interpret the experience as a past life, when in fact it might be a present one and, what's more, one shared by all of us, whether we are aware of it or not. We are all each other.

I have great respect for physicists, even though most of the time I only half understand what they are getting at – if even that. So it's a relief to realise that it is possible to discover, on ones own, at least a rudimentary understanding of the world we're in, and often be led there by the most unexpected of agents – such as, for instance, a disdainful pheasant, assorted little birds, and a black cat.

Acknowledgements

My grateful thanks to Ivan Tyrrell, Director of Human Givens College, for making available a page in each issue of the *Human Givens* Journal for me to write what I pleased; to Denise Winn, brilliant editor of that journal, with whom I had an agreement that she would not edit or change what I had written, but whose restrained suggestions, in any case, often came to my rescue; and to David Pendlebury, whose gentle mumbles and clear, kind eye on the majority of these 'Pages' was in every instance helpful.

Pat continues to write her column in the journal:
Human Givens: promoting emotional health and clear thinking.

Each issue of *Human Givens: promoting emotional health and clear thinking* is packed full of fascinating stories, research findings, new insights, articles, interviews, case histories, research, book reviews and letters (we do not take advertising). The official journal of the Human Givens Institute and ETSI, it provides much of the best writing on human psychology and behaviour currently available.

Published biannually, *Human Givens* continually explores the significance of new knowledge about human psychology, biology and behaviour wherever it has an impact on people's lives – for instance, in the areas of health, welfare, education, work, family life, communication, business and the law – and looks in detail at how people are using this knowledge to improve the effectiveness of their work, whatever their field of expertise.

To keep up with Pat's work, and discover some of the best writing on human psychology and behaviour currently available, subscribe to *Human Givens* by visiting:

humangivens.com/publications/journal-subscription

or calling:
+44 (0) 1323 811690

Human Givens
Publishing

How can we best approach the psychological pressures of living in our modern world... ?

There is currently much uncertainty among professionals and politicians about the best way to approach the psychological problems of living in our modern world: how best to educate our children; help unsocialised young adults; treat the rising rates of anxiety and depression; work with addicts; and grapple with the chaotic consequences of broken families, etc.

A new organising idea

Whenever there is widespread uncertainty like this, a new 'organising idea' is usually needed, to bring clarity and a wider perspective to the issues. An organising idea plays an active role in shaping perception, thinking and research, and is always big enough to encompass and create a context for earlier ideas which may have tackled problems piecemeal.

The human givens approach is a new organising idea founded on a solid basis of fundamental research. It is driven by our ever increasing scientific knowledge about human biology, behaviour and psychology – and an interest in how best to put such knowledge to practical use.

The approach, which initially focused on the treatment of mental distress, is rapidly being recognised as a profoundly important shift in our understanding of human functioning. It has been called "the missing heart of positive psychology".

The startling success produced by the efficacy, adaptability and practical nature of the ideas encompassed in it are borne out by the speed at which it is being used in new areas, ranging from education, physical health care, psychotherapy and social work to international diplomatic relations and the corporate world of business.

Find out more at
www.humangivens.com

What are the human givens?

Human givens are what we are all born with: our essential biological and emotional needs and the innate resources that we have evolved in order to fulfill them.

Our fundamental emotional needs are:

- Security – safe territory and an environment which allows us to develop fully
- Attention (to give and receive it) – a form of nutrition
- Sense of autonomy and control – having volition to make responsible choices
- Being emotionally connected with others
- Feeling part of a wider community
- Friendship, intimacy – to know that at least one other person accepts us totally for who we are, "warts 'n' all"
- Privacy – opportunity to reflect and consolidate experience
- Sense of status within social groupings
- Sense of competence and achievement (from which comes self-esteem)
- Meaning and purpose – which come from being stretched in what we do and think

The resources nature gave us to help us meet our needs include:

- The ability to develop complex, long-term memory, which enables us to add to our innate knowledge and learn
- The ability to build rapport, empathise and connect with others
- Imagination, which enables us to focus our attention away from our emotions, use language and problem solve more creatively and objectively
- A conscious, rational mind that can check out emotions, question, analyse and plan
- The ability to 'know' – that is, understand the world unconsciously through metaphorical pattern matching
- An observing self – that part of us that can step back, be more objective and be aware of itself as a unique centre of awareness, apart from intellect, emotion and conditioning
- A dreaming brain that preserves the integrity of our genetic inheritance every night by metaphorically defusing expectations held in the autonomic arousal system because they were not acted out the previous day.

Further Information

*If you are interested to learn more about the human givens approach, please visit **www.humangivens.com***

You might also like to know about the following:

The Human Givens Institute (HGI)

The Human Givens Institute (HGI) is both a membership organisation – open to anyone wishing to support and promote the human givens approach through all forms of psychological, educational and social interactions – and the professional body representing the interests of those in the caring, welfare and teaching professions who work in alignment with the best scientific knowledge available about the givens of human nature. For more details, visit **www.hgi.org.uk** or call **+44 (0)1323 811662**

The Human Givens College

Human Givens College provides effective psychotherapy training on the best ways to treat mental health and behavioural problems for anyone wishing to help improve the lives of individuals and families, or to help organisations and communities thrive. For full details, including information about the Human Givens Diploma Course, please visit **www.humangivens.com/college** or call the College on **+44 (0)1323 811690.**

Register of human givens therapists

For details of all fully qualified human givens therapists working in private practice, and information about how human givens psychotherapists and counsellors can help, visit **www.hgi.org.uk/therapist-register/about-register** or call **+44 (0)1323 811662.**

More books by
Human Givens Publishing

Human Givens: The new approach to
emotional health and clear thinking
Joe Griffin and Ivan Tyrrell

Listening to Idries Shah
Ivan Tyrrell

Why we dream: the definitive answer
Joe Griffin and Ivan Tyrrell

Godhead: The Brain's Big Bang:
The explosive origin of creativity, mysticism and mental illness
Joe Griffin and Ivan Tyrrell

How to Master Anxiety – all you need to know to overcome stress,
panic attacks, phobias, trauma, obsessions and more
Joe Griffin and Ivan Tyrrell

How to lift depression... fast
Joe Griffin and Ivan Tyrrell

Managing The Monkey: How to defuse the conflicts
that can lead to violence in the workplace
Mark Dawes and Denise Winn

Freedom from addiction –
the secret behind successful addiction busting
Joe Griffin and Ivan Tyrrell

For more books, CDs, MP3s and journal back issues, visit
www.humangivens.com/publications